WARWICKSHIRE'S BUTTERFLIES

Their Habitats and Where to Find Them

(Including Day-Flying Moths)

By
Keith Warmington and Margaret Vickery

Butterfly Conservation — Warwickshire Branch

Text by
Margaret Vickery, Keith Warmington, David Brown, Phil Parr and Steven Falk

Additional contributions from
Dave Cole, Jon Holmes, Richard Lamb, Roy Ledbury, Helen Newell, Jane O'Dell, Phil Pain, Ted Read, Iain Reid, John Roberts and Mike Slater

*****

Photography by
John Roberts and Keith Warmington

Additional photography by
David Brown, Jim Porter, Steven Falk, Heather Warmington and Daniel L. Warwood

Published By
The Warwickshire Branch of Butterfly Conservation

First published 2003 by Warwickshire Branch of Butterfly Conservation.

Warwickshire Branch of Butterfly Conservation
30 New Street
Baddesley Ensor
Atherstone
Warwickshire
CV9 2DW

ISBN 0-9544701-0-9

Copyright © Warwickshire Branch of Butterfly Conservation, 2003.

Copyright in the photographs remains with the individual photographers.

British Library-in-Publication Data.
A catalogue record for this book is available from the British Library.

All rights reserved. No part of the publication may be reproduced, stored in a retrieval system, or transmitted, in any form or by means electronic, mechanical, photocopying, recording or otherwise, without prior permission from the publishers.

The views expressed in this book are those of the writers.

Cover photograph: *Small Blue at Bishops Hill by Keith Warmington.*

Production and design by
Keith Warmington, 30 New Street, Baddesley Ensor, Atherstone, Warwickshire CV9 2DW.
www.warmies.co.uk

Printed in Hong Kong. The Hanway Press, London.

CONTENTS

Acknowledgements   ii
Foreword   iii
Dedication   iv

Introduction   1
    Warwickshire's Habitats   1
    Warwickshire's Butterflies   5
    Distribution Map Details   6

Woodland   7
    Mature Broad-leaved Woodland   8
    Rides, Glades and Clearings   12

Grassland   17
    Unimproved Grassland   18
    Neutral and Acid Meadows   19
    Limestone Grassland   20
    Damp Grassland and Meadows   21
    Identification Comparison: Common Blue and Brown Argus   26

Man-Made Habitats   27
    Hedgerows and Roadside Verges   28
    Field Margins and Headlands   33
    Disused Railway Lines   34
    Gardens   40
    Warwickshire's Garden Butterfly survey   41
    Parks and Urban Habitats   44
    Churchyards   49
    Industrial and Post-Industrial Landscape   54

Day-Flying Moths   59
    Introduction   60
    Woodland   61
    Neutral and Acid Grassland   63
    Limestone Grassland   65
    Wetlands   67
    Gardens and Parks   69
    Heathland   70

Appendix One   Distribution Status of Butterflies in Warwickshire   72
Appendix Two   Butterfly Plants   73
Appendix Three   Gazetteer   74
Appendix Four   Butterfly Conservation   76
Appendix Five   Further Information   77

Index of Warwickshire's Butterflies   78
Index of Warwickshire's Day-Flying Moths   79

ACKNOWLEDGEMENTS

Warwickshire Branch of Butterfly Conservation gratefully acknowledges the financial support of the following organisations and individuals. Without their generous donations this publication would not have been possible.

North Warwickshire Borough Council
Atherstone Natural History Society
Heart of England Co-Operative Society (Helping Hearts)
Barclays Bank
Stratford Butterfly Farm
Focus Optics Ltd
Warwickshire Museum

Russ Allen
Maurice Arnold
Trevor Bailey
June M. Birnie
David Brown
Beryl E. Collinge
W.M.S. Dugdale
Steven Falk
Alma Faulkner
Loraine & David Harding
Val Hill
Elizabeth Hodgkin
Chris Johnson
Molly Kearns
Emily Marie Kirk
Margaret Kirk
Richard Lamb
Roy Ledbury
John Liggins
Phil Pain
Phil Parr

Dave Porter
Kath Randall
John Reeve
Celia & Dave Rickers
John & Val Roberts
L. Rover
Elaine M. Rumary
Mike Slater
Mark Smith
Chris & Gill Toney
C. Tyler-Smith
F.W. Tunbridge
Margaret Vickery
Keith & Heather Warmington
Christine M. Warmington
Robin & Margaret Warwood
Val Weston
Mike Williams
J. Wills
Mrs V.H. Youell

Special thanks to Rob Still for his technical advice and support, to Steven Falk for his proof reading and enthusiasm for the project and to all the people who have provided butterfly records over the years.

FOREWORD

The significance of this book is manifold. It is an important achievement by a dynamic and well-organised local branch of Butterfly Conservation. The potential of enthusiastic volunteers for contributing to our understanding and conservation of biodiversity should never be under-estimated!

It also flags the conservation issues and challenges currently facing Warwickshire's butterflies. These include the protection and management of our better butterfly sites, the creation of new butterfly habitat, the possible reintroduction of key species and the promotion of butterflies as something worth celebrating by society in general.

It may not go unnoticed that many of our scarcer species occur within old quarries, disused railway lines and old industrial sites. Most of these sites fall into the category of previously developed or 'brown-field' land, a land category we are constantly being urged to develop in favour of 'green-field' land. This book demonstrates the dangerous over-simplification of this approach, and the high conservation value of certain individual brown-field sites for butterflies.

But the conservation of Warwickshire's butterflies is by no means a narrow, blinkered endeavour. Butterflies are a wonderful flagship group. Their favoured sites are shared by many other attractive or unusual animals and plants. Conserving our few remaining populations of Small Blue, Dingy Skipper and Green Hairstreak will automatically confer benefit on a much larger assemblage of other insects and wildflowers.

Let us hope that this book will not only mark a turning point in the fortune of Warwickshire's scarcer butterflies but also help to celebrate the familiar ones too.

Steven Falk
Senior Keeper of Natural History
Warwickshire Museum

White-letter Hairstreak — *John Roberts*

> *The study of butterflies - creatures selected as the types of airiness and frivolity - instead of being despised, will some day be valued as one of the most important branches of biological science.*
>
> *Henry Walter Bates*
> *Naturalist and Explorer*
> *1825-1892*

This book is dedicated to all who care for our Warwickshire butterflies.

Introduction

There has to be habitat before there can be butterflies. This is a truism that conservation volunteers know only too well! So this book is based on habitats and their associated butterflies. There is more than one way to classify habitat, but we have divided this book into three main sections, echoing the three main habitat types found in Warwickshire: Woodland, Unimproved Grassland and Man-made Habitats. Within each section will be found secondary habitat types such as woodland glades or limestone grassland. Of course it can be argued that every habitat type in Warwickshire is now man-made, after thousands of years of human occupation and interference, but in the woodlands and unimproved grasslands where butterflies breed, nature has the upper hand, whereas in the man-made section man and nature are working in partnership.

Reading about butterflies and their habitats is only part of the experience, you need to be able to see the reality, and so we have included many sites which you can visit and where you can see Warwickshire's butterflies in their natural surroundings. For those new to the delights of butterfly watching, just remember to check the flight times (included under each species' map) if you are hoping to see a particular species, and chose a warm, sunny day for your visit.

Although butterflies can often be seen in the evening, particularly, the Purple and White-letter Hairstreaks, most species are more likely to be seen in late morning or the afternoon.

Warwickshire's Habitats

Warwickshire, situated in the heart of England, is a county of gentle hills and valleys with a moderate climate. The abundant coal seams point to the occurrence, about 300 million years ago, of dense sub-tropical forests of giant horsetails and tree ferns. A remnant of this era remains in the horsetails, no bigger than a stinging nettle, which are present in the county today. The geology of the county is varied and both sandstone and Blue Lias clay, which contains limestone, are present, influencing the plant life and, hence, the butterfly species breeding in the county.

After the last ice age, succession through grassland and scrub led eventually to the 'wildwood', which must have covered most of the county. Long before the Roman invasion, Warwickshire inhabitants had cleared large areas of wildwood and by the time of the Domesday Book in 1086 only about 20% of the county was wooded.

View of Warwickshire from Burton Dassett Hills — Keith Warmington

After the devastation of the Black Death in the 1300's, woodland started to regenerate and expand naturally to regain some of its lost ground, although only about 3% of the county is wooded today. Wood was an important commodity and managing woodlands as coppice with standards became the norm.

Snitterfield Wood, South Warwickshire — John Roberts

Coppicing opened up large woodland glades to sunlight, while the removal of the cut wood in carts would have resulted in sunny rides. Butterflies took advantage of these sunny, sheltered habitats and it must have been a glorious sight to see the fritillaries and other species nectaring on the abundant wild flowers, which would have thrived in such situations. During the 20th century, especially after the second world war, coppice management was abandoned and many woods in Warwickshire were clear felled and planted with conifers. Softwoods are quick growing and so profitable, but mature trees planted close together let no light onto the forest floor, which is bereft of both flowers and butterflies. Transitory populations of both may appear after clear felling such forests, but soon die out again when new trees shade the ground once more. With cheap imports of wood, today such forests are gradually reverting to broadleaved woodlands again, but some have been lost forever under roads, housing estates etc. Both Ryton and Hampton Woods are good examples of Warwickshire woods brought back to coppice with standards management. In Ryton Wood, the Silver-washed Fritillary can once again be seen nectaring on bramble blossom. If the whole Pincethorpe complex of woodland to which it belongs could be brought back to this type of management, a daunting but not impossible task, then one day it may be possible to see again Pearl-bordered and Small Pearl-bordered Fritillaires amongst the violets.

The Enclosures Acts (1720 - 1880) resulted in many miles of hedging appearing in Warwickshire and on maturity the many elm trees included in these hedges gave the county its name of Leafy Warwickshire. Alas, this is no longer true. Many hedges were destroyed in the latter part of the last century to produce large, economical fields and Dutch Elm disease has devastated the elms. Soil erosion soon showed the error of removing hedges and hopefully, government grants to plant new ones will eventually result once again in a 'leafy Warwickshire'.

Oxhouse Farm — John Roberts

In medieval times flower meadows which were cut for hay to feed the animals in winter were plentiful and an extremely valuable commodity. The variety and abundance of nectar flowers and larval foodplants, including fine grasses, growing in these meadows attracted many butterfly species. Alas, silage became a more important food source for cattle in winter and this is best made with grass alone - 'weeds' are not welcome! Most of the hay meadows have been ploughed and reseeded with coarse grasses, either for silage or for grazing. Such 'improved' grassland, fed with fertilizers and kept free of wild flowers with herbicides, is of little use to butterflies or most other wildlife, and much of Warwickshire is now little more than an impoverished green desert.

There are a few remnants of the old hay meadows still surviving, such as Draycote Meadow, and most are now Warwickshire Wildlife Trust reserves and thus protected from destruction.

Warwickshire once contained extensive areas of heathland and wetland.

In the Middle Ages there were many acres of heathland on the sandy soils, but today the only area of any size is that at Sutton Park, which has been protected from development. Specialised heathland butterflies no longer occur; the Silver-studded Blue, for example, has been extinct in the county for a hundred years or more.

Flood plains along the rivers resulted in seasonal wetland where damp-loving butterflies, such as the Orange Tip, would have thrived. Drainage for agriculture and building has destroyed many such wetland areas, but patches still exist, such as those at Eathorpe, Temple Balsall, Whitacre Heath and Welches Meadow in Leamington, which has been reinstated as permanent wetland. There are also quite extensive areas of man-made wetland at Brandon Marsh Nature Reserve, Kingsbury Water Park and Draycote Reservoir, all areas that are home to a variety of butterfly species.

Man-made habitats have developed mainly from disused coal mines, quarries and railway lines. Coal mines with their associated spoil tips have had a dramatic effect on the scenery and wildlife of North Warwickshire. The black coloured soil absorbs heat quickly and remains warm for longer than lighter coloured soils. This creates a warm microclimate, which attracts the Wall and Dingy Skipper butterflies.

The disused limestone quarries in the south and east of the county have become colonised by alkaline soil-loving plants. This, together with their often sheltered aspects, supports limestone grassland butterfly species, such as the Small Blue.

Disused railway lines quickly revert to scrubland if not actively managed, and then attract few butterflies.

However, railway cuttings which are kept open through the work of conservation volunteers or rabbit grazing, are often much warmer and more sheltered than their surroundings and become home to many species of both butterfly and moth. Those in deep cuttings can be especially good. The Green Hairstreak is a characteristic species of such habitats.

Gardens already cover much of Warwickshire and are likely to increase their acreage in years to come.

Both gardens and parks can be made into valuable butterfly and moth habitats and Butterfly Conservation can offer advice and literature on how to do this to best effect. This is a way in which all lovers of these insects can help to support many species, although there will always be those whose needs are so specialised that they will never move from natural habitat to parks or gardens.

Warwickshire's Butterflies

There are 33 species of butterfly breeding in Warwickshire today, but not all are found throughout the county. Some, such as the Peacock and Small Tortoiseshell, whose caterpillars feed on stinging nettles, can be found almost anywhere, but others, such as Small Blue, Grizzled Skipper and Silver-washed Fritillary have a very restricted range. Such restrictions can be due to the rarity of the larval foodplant, as with kidney vetch for the Small Blue; a need for a particular type of habitat - woodland with open, sunny rides for the Silver-washed Fritillary - or a combination of both.

The Grizzled Skipper needs habitat which is both sheltered and sunny and contains wild strawberry plants in abundance.

Grizzled Skipper (photo: Keith Warmington)

The most widespread species found in both the countryside and parks and gardens, include Comma, Peacock, Small Tortoiseshell and Red Admiral (all of whose larvae are stinging nettle feeders), Large, Small and Green-veined Whites, Meadow Brown, Gatekeeper, Brimstone, Holly Blue and Painted Lady.

Rarer visitors to gardens, but which can be seen over a wide area of Warwickshire, include Orange Tip (needs a moist habitat), Ringlet (a hedge and woodland species), Common Blue

Common Blue mating (photo: Keith Warmington)

(grassland); Large and Small Skipper (grassland), and Speckled Wood (woodland). Species with specialised requirements include Marbled White (limestone grassland), White Admiral (shady woodland), White-letter Hairstreak (elms) and Purple Hairstreak (oaks).

There are also other factors we know little about which effect species distribution, such as microclimate and the presence or absence of parasites and predators. In the short term weather is also an important factor for good or ill and its effects can often last several years. However, the most important variable in maintaining a butterfly species is an extensive area of suitable habitat, and in Warwickshire, as in most other counties, such habitats are fragmented and disappearing at an alarming rate. This is due both to intensive farming practices and through the construction of roads, houses, shops and factories etc.

Pearl-bordered and Small Pearl-bordered Fritillaries have become extinct in Warwickshire because there is insufficient coppiced woodland in the county now to support permanent colonies of these species.

Small Pearl-bordered Fritillary — Keith Warmington

The Duke of Burgundy Fritillary hung on in a small area of Warwickshire for many years but finally died out in the 1990s, most probably due to insufficient suitable habitat.

Duke of Burgundy Fritillary — Keith Warmington

Sometimes species are able to adapt to a different habitat and/or larval foodplant, but such populations are too small to maintain the adaptation when conditions are bad. A recent example of this was the sudden expansion of Brown Argus in Warwickshire, with the larvae feeding on doves-foot cranesbill instead of the usual rockrose. This lasted for about three years, but a series of poor summers seems to have wiped out these new populations, which never consisted of more than a few individuals.

Warwickshire Wildlife Trust, Butterfly Conservation and several of our Local Authorities are working to protect and maintain existing butterfly and moth habitats in the Warwickshire sub region and wherever possible to create new ones. It is a long and laborious process but the joy of seeing these beautiful insects flitting among the flowers is reward enough for such effort.

Distribution Maps

The maps showing the distribution of each butterfly species in Warwickshire are produced from data collected for 'The Butterflies for the New Millennium Project', a survey of the distribution of butterflies in Britain and Ireland between 1995 and 1999 organized jointly by Butterfly Conservation and the Biological Record Centre. The results of the survey have been summarised to provide the core of the superbly illustrated book 'The Millennium Atlas of Butterflies in Britain and Ireland'.

The Warwickshire data covers all of the 705 tetrads (2km x 2km squares) that make up the old Vice County 38 that is Warwickshire and parts of the West Midlands (Coventry, Solihull and parts of modern Birmingham).

Some 220 volunteer butterfly recorders recorded a total of 64,629 butterfly sightings over the five year period and every one of the 705 tetrads was surveyed for butterflies.

A minimum of 10 species has been recorded from each tetrad and two tetrads have recorded a maximum of 31 species.

The data from the 'Butterflies for the New Millennium Project' forms a baseline of detailed data for fresh ideas, better methods and increased activity in the recording, monitoring, research and conservation of butterflies in the new millennium.

WOODLAND

Silver-washed Fritillary   *Keith Warmington*

Mature Broad-Leaved Woodland

Ryton Wood, Nr Coventry — John Roberts

The deciduous forest made up of small-leaved lime, elm, oak, ash, alder and birch which covered Warwickshire after the end of the last ice age is now almost entirely gone. A photograph of Warwickshire taken from space today would show it to be one of the least wooded counties with only about 3% of the land surface covered in woodland. In Shakespeare's time woodland was much more extensive, especially in the west (Ancient Arden). Even 60 years ago the number of trees in woods and hedges lent credence to the county's nickname of 'Leafy Warwickshire'. Since then, modern farming methods have seen the removal of hedges, and Dutch Elm disease has ravaged the elms in those that were left. Many of the

Silver-washed Fritillary *Argynnis paphia*

The largest and most spectacular of the British fritillaries, the Silver-washed Fritillary is named after the silver streaks on the underside of the hind wing which can be viewed as it stops to feed on flowers such as bramble.

The male has a powerful gliding flight and can often be seen jostling for nectar on bramble patches.

Although the butterfly is seen in the sunny glades and rides of woodland, it actually breeds in the shadier parts where it lays it's eggs on the base of a tree trunk where dog-violets grow. woodland floor.

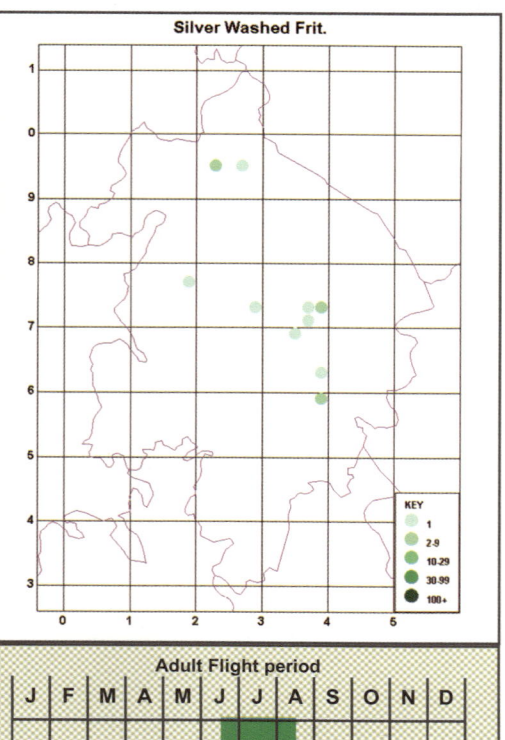

Silver Washed Frit.

KEY: 1, 2-9, 10-29, 30-99, 100+

Adult Flight period

| J | F | M | A | M | J | J | A | S | O | N | D |

White Admiral *Limenitis camilla*

The White Admiral is a spectacular woodland butterfly, with white-banded, dark chocolate-brown wings.

This butterfly, as it travels through the dappled sunlight of open woodland glades in search of bramble flowers, exhibits a distinctive delicate flight with short periods of wing beats followed by long glides.

It is a fairly shade-tolerant butterfly, flying in overgrown and partially shaded woodland to lay eggs on honeysuckle.

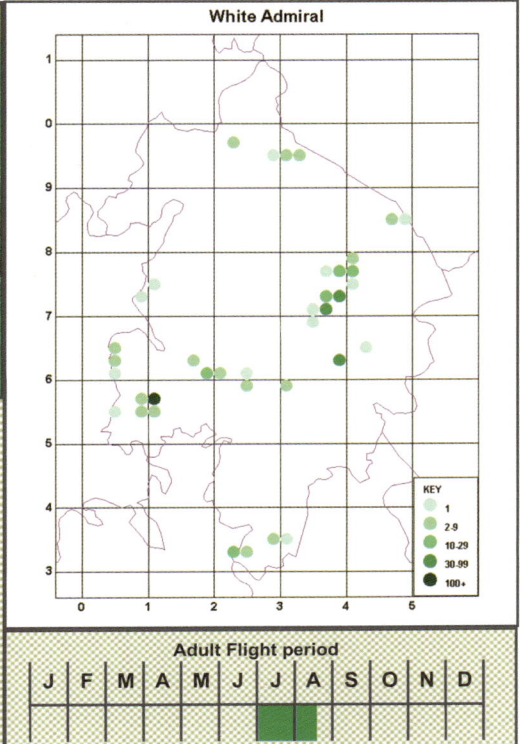

remaining woods were clear felled and planted with conifers, which grow much more quickly than hardwoods. Although newly planted conifer plantations can support a good variety of wildlife, including butterflies, as the closely packed trees grow they shade out other plants so that little can survive. Eventually the area becomes an impoverished habitat completely inhospitable to butterflies. The remaining hardwood plantations also became less attractive to butterflies as active management ceased, particularly following the second world war, and trees and bramble swamped out rides and clearings. One butterfly, the White Admiral, prefers habitats in which its foodplant, honeysuckle, grows in shaded areas and this species has thrived in Warwickshire, especially during the last quarter of the 20th century. It is now found in many woods across the county. However, this has been at the expense of the woodland fritillaries, all of which have become extinct in the county except for a small re-introduced colony of Silver-washed Fritillary based in Ryton Wood. Violets are the caterpillar foodplant of the Silver-washed Fritillary and in Ryton Wood, management aims to encourage the growth of violets in a habitat suitable for these butterflies.

However, not all is doom and gloom, as in the last quarter of the 20th century Warwickshire Wildlife Trust (WWT) volunteers took on the management of several large woodlands using the well established method of coppice with standards. They have succeeded in producing several woods in which up to 31 species of butterfly can be seen. WWT is the largest woodland owner but others such as Forest Enterprise, private owners and county and local councils followed their lead, so that most of the best woodlands in the county are now actively managed. A good butterfly wood has a diverse, uneven structure, with some tall, mature trees (standards) and some regrowth (coppice) at a mixture of heights, together with open, sunny rides and glades. Add to this unshaded bare areas of cleared vegetation and others in which abundant wild flowers grow and you have a perfect habitat for woodland butterflies. It is probably true to say that in such a woodland in Warwickshire you will see more species of butterfly than in any other type of habitat. Such well-managed woods are home to a vast range of other wildlife too, including rare and threatened species. They are a delight to visit all year round and a valuable resource for the future of Warwickshire's wildlife.

It is largely thanks to English Nature and Warwickshire Wildlife Trust that most of the best woodlands in Warwickshire are either nature reserves, SSSI's or both. The complex of woodlands in the Princethorpe area is particularly important as these woods are remnants of ancient woodland and cover a large area. Ryton, Wappenbury, Waverley, Bubbenhall and Princethorpe Great Wood are magnificent woods whose linking would create a huge tract of woodland not seen in Warwickshire for hundreds of years.

Such ancient woodlands date back at least four centuries and have been home to thousands of plant, animal and insect species. These species are the source for woodlands being newly created today. However, to ensure the spread of species into new areas there must be wildlife corridors from one wood to another, such as hedgerows, flower rich grasslands, road verges and field margins, canals and rivers.

The ancient woods of Warwickshire vary in their character depending on the underlying soils. In the northwest the soil is more acidic and less fertile than that in the southeast, which is alkaline. Trees characteristic of acidic soils, such as those found in the Princethorpe complex of woodlands, include sessile oak, small-leaved lime and silver and downy birch, with an understorey of bracken, holly, rowan and buckthorn, the latter the foodplant of the Brimstone butterfly. Other woods with this characteristic assemblage of plants include Kingsbury, Sutton Park, Hartshill Hayes and Windmill Naps in the north, while in the mid-region there is Piles Coppice and Brandon Wood, east of Coventry and Crackley Wood near Kenilworth. Ash is the predominant tree of alkaline soils and the understorey contains Midland hawthorn, dogwood, wayfaring tree.

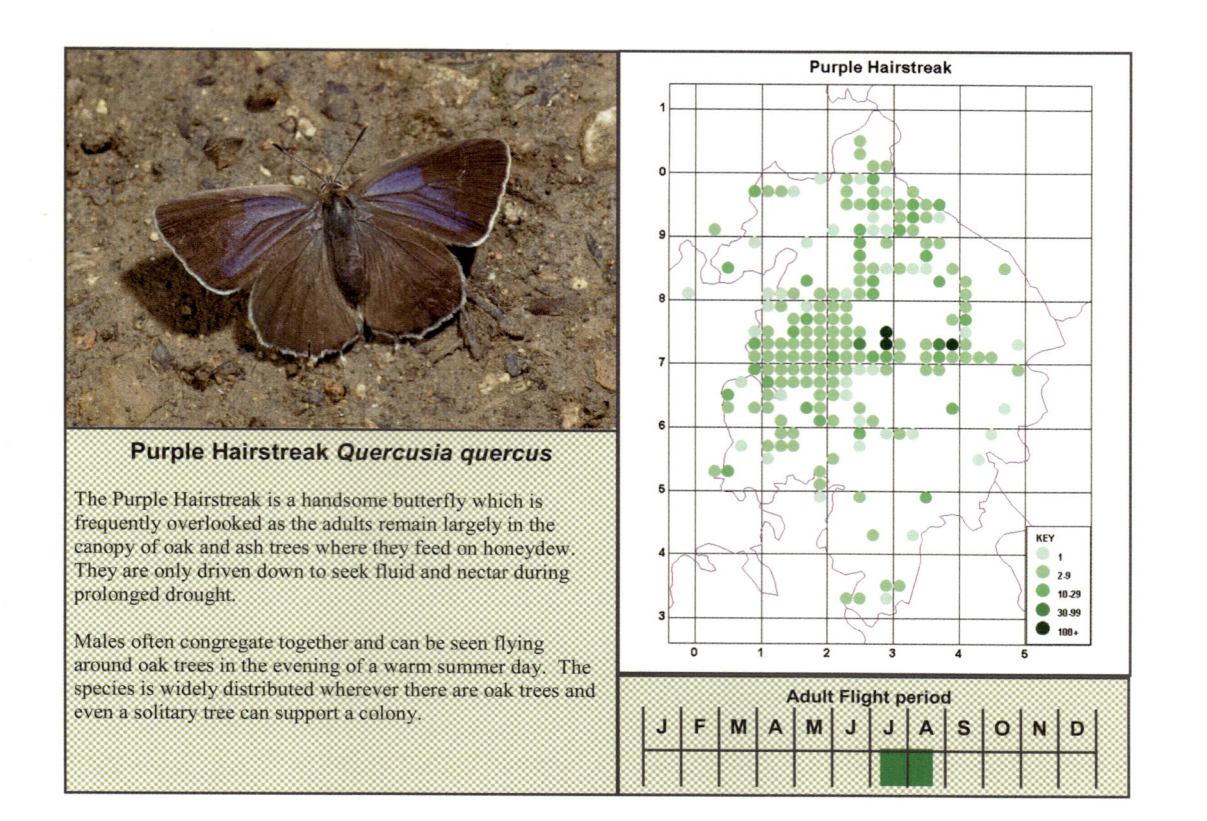

Purple Hairstreak *Quercusia quercus*

The Purple Hairstreak is a handsome butterfly which is frequently overlooked as the adults remain largely in the canopy of oak and ash trees where they feed on honeydew. They are only driven down to seek fluid and nectar during prolonged drought.

Males often congregate together and can be seen flying around oak trees in the evening of a warm summer day. The species is widely distributed wherever there are oak trees and even a solitary tree can support a colony.

Wood White *Leptidea sinapis*

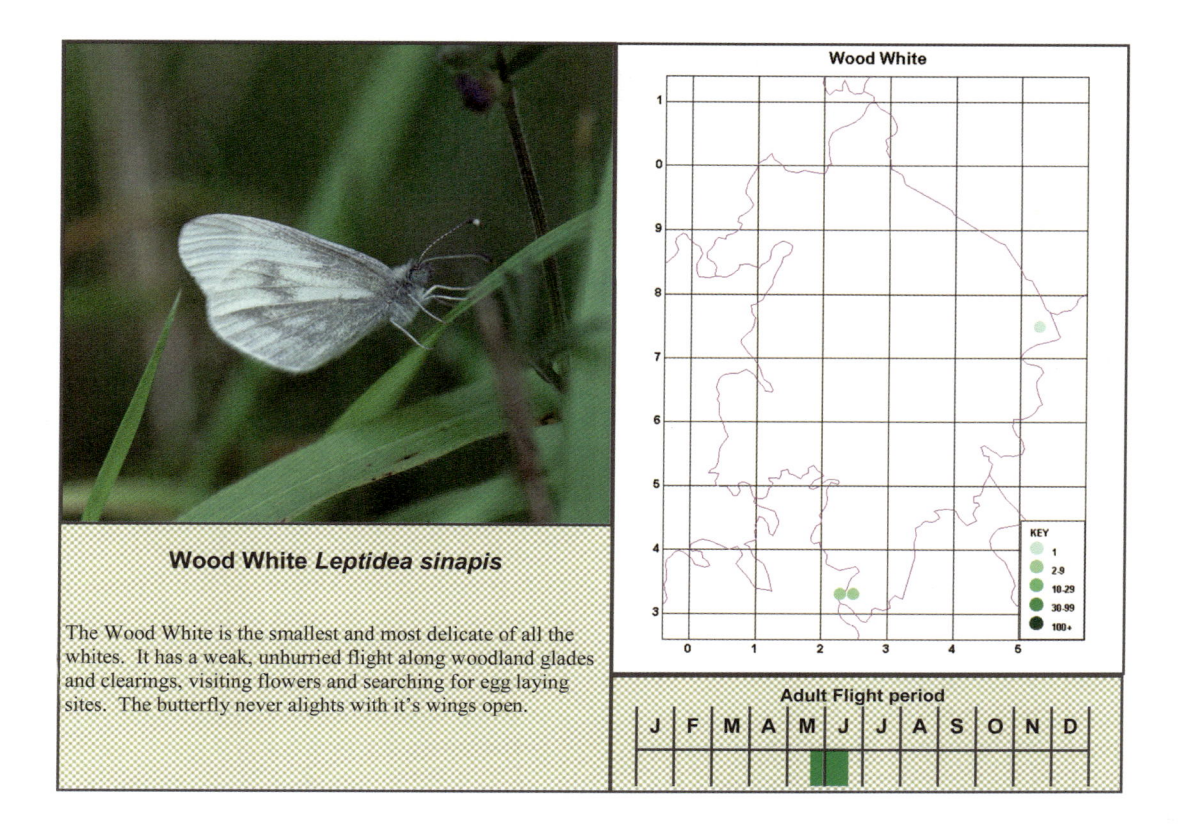

The Wood White is the smallest and most delicate of all the whites. It has a weak, unhurried flight along woodland glades and clearings, visiting flowers and searching for egg laying sites. The butterfly never alights with it's wings open.

Woodlands showing these vegetation characteristics include Snitterflield Bushes, Ufton Wood, Oversley Wood and on the Oxfordshire border, Whichford and Wolford Woods, the latter containing the only known colony of Wood White remaining in Warwickshire.

When correctly managed, ancient woodlands produce a rich and varied ground flora, with ample nectar plants for butterflies, as well as essential caterpillar foodplants. Several woodland butterflies have very specific caterpillar food plants for example, honeysuckle for the White Admiral, violets for the Fritillaries and oaks for the Purple Hairstreak. Should active management cease, shading will occur as the young trees grow and both flowers and butterflies decline. The development of shade after active management ceased in Warwickshire woods during the twentieth century was the main cause of the extinction of most of the woodland fritillaries.

Val and I were walking past Print Wood searching successfully for White-letter Hairstreaks, when further along the track an entirely unclothed man appeared, coming towards us. He seemed to be peering at bramble flowers....possibly with the same quarry as ourselves?

There is no social etiquette for such encounters and as we hastily devised one he looked up, spotted us and in a twinkling vanished into the prickly undergrowth never to be seen again.

John Roberts

Rides, Glades and Clearings

We speak of woodland butterflies, but except for a few species it is not among the trees that we find these insects, the environment is too cold and dark. Even those butterflies associated with denser woodland, such as Purple and White-letter Hairstreak, are not found beneath the canopy at ground level but are seen flying amongst the tops in sunlight.

Woodland butterflies are mainly found in sunny rides, glades and clearings. Rides and clearings are man-made and maintained, the former once constructed for the benefit of huntsmen (hence the name, 'rides'), but now to facilitate the removal of timber. Clearings are the result of clear felling an area of trees and can be valuable butterfly habitat for a short time, until newly planted trees or natural regrowth shades out the opportunistic wild flowers and grasses. Natural glades are usually the small open areas that result from the falling of a tree or the encroachment of woodland onto older grassland. The best rides and clearings are those with a range of flowery vegetation, including unimproved grassland, tall herb, bramble fringes and blossoming scrub such as sallow or hawthorn. In the absence of human management deer and rabbit grazing can be crucial in maintaining their value for butterflies.

Almost all Warwickshire's butterfly species can be found in rides, glades and clearings. Even White Admiral adults prefer to nectar on thistles or bramble here, though they lay eggs on honeysuckle in more shaded areas. Many species generally associated with grassland are found in these open spaces, including Dingy and Grizzled Skipper, Brown Argus, Common Blue, Marbled White, Ringlet and Meadow Brown. One of the most delightful experiences is to see a Silver-washed Fritillary gliding from one bramble bush to another along a sunny ride, nectaring on the flowers as it goes.

Comma *Polygonia c-album*

The Comma is a distinctive butterfly when seen closely with it's ragged, torn outline, rich orange upperside and the white 'comma' shape on the underside of it's forewing. When hibernating it becomes virtually impossible to detect amongst withered brown leaves.

Although a regular visitor to garden buddleia it favours woodland glades where it dashes and glides, fritillary-like in search of bramble flowers and fermenting blackberry fruits.

Ringlet *Aphantopus hyperantus*

A newly emerged male Ringlets has a deep, velvety almost black appearance which fades to brown after a few days exposure to the sun. It has a white fringe to the wings and the small circles on the underwings, which give the butterfly it's name, vary in number and size and may be enlarged and elongated or reduced to small white spots which occasionally lack the black ring.

Ringlets particularly favour the damp, shady grassland that is found along the edge of woodland rides and glades.

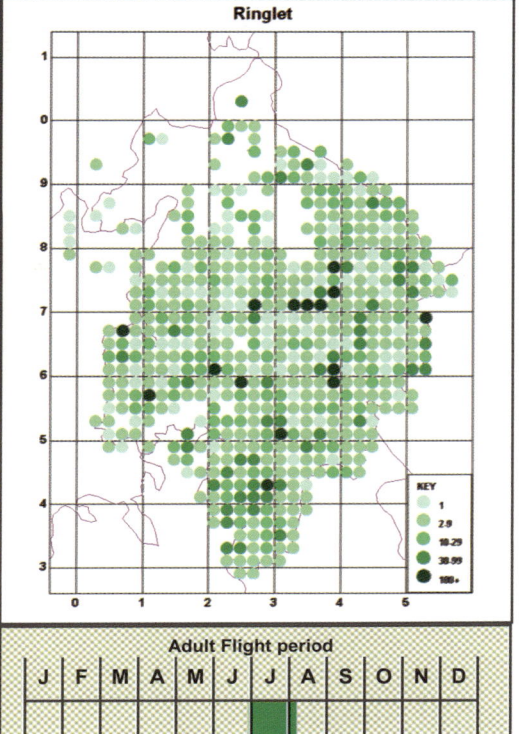

Recommended Sites:

Ryton Wood Nature Reserve
(SP384726)

Owned by Warwickshire Wildlife Trust, this is probably the wood with the greatest number of resident butterfly species. It is an SSSI and a remnant of very old woodland with some coppiced small-leaved lime trees thought to originate in the 1400s. It seems likely that some parts of the wood date back to the time of the Doomsday Book. 30 species of butterfly have been recorded in the period 1995 -2000, including Silver-washed Fritillary, White Admiral, Essex Skipper, Dingy Skipper, Marbled White and Purple Hairstreak and White-letter Hairstreak. Ryton Wood is also a good habitat for moths and contains a wealth of wild flowers, particularly in spring when bluebells, violets, primroses and wood anemones bloom.

Ryton Wood lies to the east of Bubbenhall and is best approached from the Ryton Pools car park using the permissive footpath. There is a small charge for parking.

Hampton Wood Nature Reserve
(SP254600)

A dedicated team of volunteers have transformed Hampton Wood from a tangle of vegetation into the well managed woodland it is today. It is a delight to walk through at any season, but particularly in spring when the primroses are in bloom. In any one year it is possible to see at least 18 species of butterfly including White Admiral, Purple Hairstreak and White-letter Hairstreak. The wood, which is owned by WWT, lies off Fulbrook Lane between Hampton Lucy and Sherbourne.

Snitterfield Bushes Nature Reserve
(SP200603)

Snitterfield Bushes, now owned by WWT, was once part of a large wood that extended to

Bearley village, but during the second world war most was felled to build an airfield. The nature reserve is the result of regrowth of trees, scrub and wild flowers after the war, probably from dormant seed in the soil, as many species present today are characteristic of ancient woodland. There is an abundance of wildlife and in spring the bluebells, primroses and orchids are a delight to see. Within the woodland there are several clearings with small populations of Grizzled Skipper (reflecting the lime-rich soils), one of Warwickshire's rarer butterfly species. Later in the year the striking White Admiral can be seen gliding among the trees.

Snitterflield Bushes NR can be approached from Snitterfield along the road to Bearley. There is a lay by for parking or WWT members can use the padlocked car park.

Additional Sites:

Hartshill Hayes Country Park (SP317943)

Although this woodland site has been clear-felled and replanted by the Forestry Commission with larch, pine and spruce, useful pockets of broad-leaved trees have survived with large oak standards and small-leaved lime coppiced stools. It is one of the best woodland site, with public access, in north Warwickshire. Notable species include White-letter Hairstreak and Purple Hairstreak and White Admiral.

Wappenbury Wood (SP381711) and Brandon Wood (SP399771)

These sites are both worth visiting and have populations of White Admiral. Wappenbury adjoins Ryton Wood and is being managed in the same way since it was acquired by WWT. Silver-washed Fritillaries have recently spread to Wappenbury from Ryton. Brandon Wood was one of the woods that was extensively clear felled and planted with conifers in the last century. However, it is slowly being restored through the efforts of the Friends of Brandon Wood and the many open areas are attractive to a number of butterfly species.

Whichford Wood (SP343296)

Found on the Oxfordshire border this woodland has public access and supports both White Admiral and Purple Hairstreak. The nearby Wolford Wood with its Wood White population is a privately owned SSSI and there is no public access.

White Admiral, Ryton Wood — Keith Warmington

Oversley Wood
(SP105563)

Oversley Wood is a working Forestry Commission woodland, roughly a mile to the south east of Alcester. It is rectangular in shape and about one and a half kilometres long by half a kilometre wide.

Access to the woodland is via a small track off the old Alcester Road that leads to a small area where cars can be parked, just under a bridge off the Alcester bypass on the north east corner of the woodland. Right around the woodland is a track with public access and there are other smaller pathways that bisect most parts of the woodland.

Although most of the woodland is mature conifer plantation, there are blocks of mature oak with associated understorey and one block of mature beech. In the south east corner there is a large plantation of young oaks with associated scrubby vegetation.

Most of the butterfly interest is associated with the wide sunny track with its grassy flower filled margins and the more open area to the south east.

In the early part of the year on a still and sunny day in February or March, the first butterflies to be encountered in Oversley are Brimstone and Comma coming out of hibernation, soon to be joined by Small Tortoiseshells and Peacocks. Later on during April and May, Orange Tips appear and depending on the stage in their abundance cycle, Holly Blues. It is at this time of year that Large, Small and Green-veined Whites are first on the wing. These species can then be found for most of the summer.

In the areas where there is open sparse vegetation during May, Dingy and Grizzled Skippers fly with the first Common Blues. Later, in August these same areas support Small Copper and Brown Argus with second generation Common Blues. Where the ground flora is richer with coarser grasses Small and Large Skippers can be found in June and July, along with plenty of Meadow Browns, Gatekeepers and Ringlets.

The partially shady tracks through the woodland are ideal for Speckled Wood which can be found from March to October. The woodland with its half shaded honeysuckle, is also ideal for White Admiral. This was so abundant one July during Millennium Atlas recording that dozens of them crashed into my bare legs as I walked around the track in my shorts. The woodland is on a small hill and the tallest trees on the top of the hill attract one of the few tree dependant species, Purple Hairstreak. This can be seen in the late afternoons of July and August.

The regular migrants that come to Oversley Wood include Red Admiral every summer, and Painted Lady in most years. These join the Peacocks and Small Tortoiseshells fuelling up on nectar in the late summer. Other species recorded in the vicinity include White Letter Hairstreak, dependant on elms suckering in the nearby hedgerows, and Marbled White and Wall Brown that prefer the more open areas of Grove Hill less than a kilometre to the south east. Oversley Wood contains a very large percentage of the butterfly species of Warwickshire and is also important for many other groups of wildlife – an interesting place to visit at any time of year.

Richard Lamb

Butterflies are the most beloved of all insects - they are perhaps the only generally beloved insects - and they rank among the most beautiful creatures in existence. The Irish believe they are the souls of the dead waiting to pass through purgatory.

Diana Ajjan

GRASSLAND

Limestone Grassland *John Roberts*

Unimproved Grassland

Unimproved grassland, Nr Corley, North Warwickshire. Keith Warmington

In centuries past much of the pasture and meadowland of Warwickshire would have been full of wildflowers and butterflies in summer. Herbicides had not been invented and fertilisation would have been much less regular and intense than today. This is called unimproved grassland. Much of this grassland was used for hay production and cut in midsummer. Often animals were put to graze on the cut areas in autumn and again in early spring.

Such meadows provided the ideal habitat for a large variety of flowering plants, including several species of orchid, and, of course, both butterfly larval foodplants and nectar plants. Yellow rattle is a plant characteristic of old hay meadows, as is birds-foot trefoil, the larval foodplant of the Common Blue. Some of the fine grasses are larval foodplants for Meadow Brown and Small and Large Skipper. Although still common as late as the 1950s, such

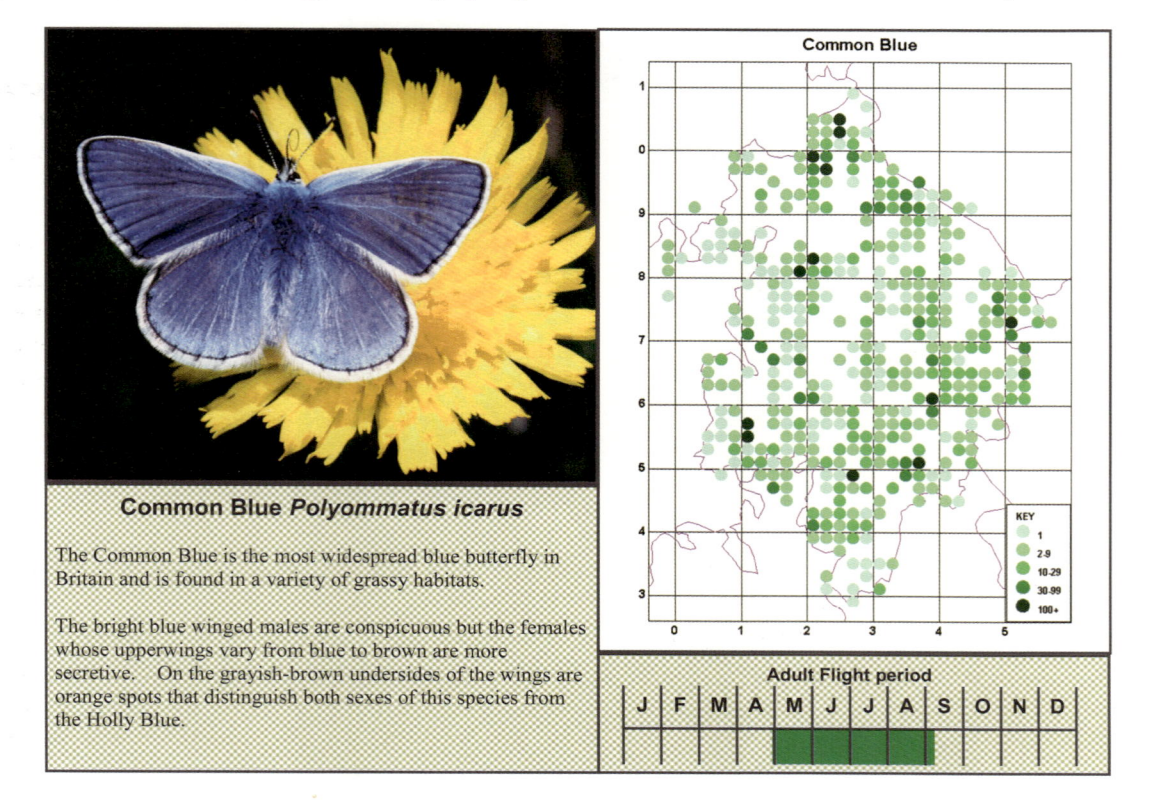

Common Blue *Polyommatus icarus*

The Common Blue is the most widespread blue butterfly in Britain and is found in a variety of grassy habitats.

The bright blue winged males are conspicuous but the females whose upperwings vary from blue to brown are more secretive. On the grayish-brown undersides of the wings are orange spots that distinguish both sexes of this species from the Holly Blue.

Brown Argus *Aricia agestis*

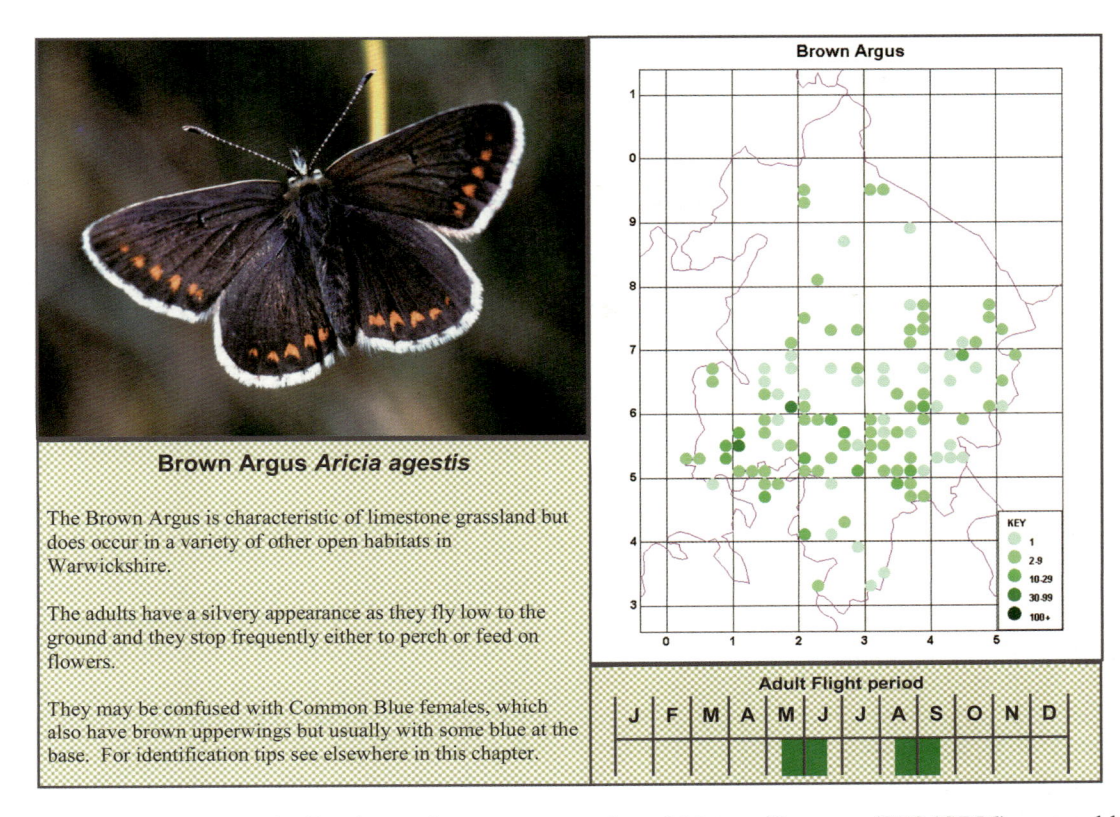

The Brown Argus is characteristic of limestone grassland but does occur in a variety of other open habitats in Warwickshire.

The adults have a silvery appearance as they fly low to the ground and they stop frequently either to perch or feed on flowers.

They may be confused with Common Blue females, which also have brown upperwings but usually with some blue at the base. For identification tips see elsewhere in this chapter.

unimproved grassland has declined to a tiny fragment today due to agricultural improvement which can invariably involve the use of fertilizers and herbicides, which kill most flowering plants. The composition of the grasses has changed too, due to the ploughing up of old grassland and reseeding with fast growing varieties that are unsuitable as larval foodplants for most butterfly species. Much of the better unimproved grassland in Warwickshire is now protected on nature reserves and Sites of Special Scientific Interest (SSSI's). Examples are Draycote Meadow (SP448706), Dean's Green (SP132682) and Shadowbrook (SP187814) Nature Reserves, all owned by Warwickshire Wildlife Trust.

Neutral and Acid Meadows

The few remaining neutral or acid meadows are thinly scattered, mostly in central, north and west Warwickshire off the limestone. Harvest Hill Nature Reserve (SP279823) in Coventry, managed by Warwickshire Wildlife Trust, still has wild daffodils and Stonebridge Meadows Local Nature Reserve (SP348756), owned by Coventry City Council is a remnant of acid meadow and floodplain grassland with harebells and pignut.

Although surrounded by dense housing, Sutton Park National Nature Reserve is relatively unchanged from the time when it was a country deer park. It still contains large areas of heathland (with heather and gorse predominating), acid grassland and valley mire of national significance. At least 21 species of butterfly have been recorded, including Green Hairstreak and Small Heath. Although devil's-bit scabious, the caterpillar foodplant of the Marsh Fritillary occurs, the butterfly, itself, became extinct many decades ago, possibly because of insufficient grazing during parts of the early 20th Century

Relatively few butterfly species occur on neutral and acid grassland in Warwickshire compared with the number which occur on calcareous grassland. Meadow Brown is one of the most common and Small Copper and Common Blue are fairly widespread. Wall has been recorded at

Limestone Grassland

Limestone grassland is one of the most important habitats for butterflies in Warwickshire. These grasslands overlie alkaline limestone where soil is either thin or non-existant. Patches of this habitat can be found in a broad band running Southwest - Northeast from The Cotswolds to Rugby with outliers in places like Wilmcote. They include several disused railway lines and many old quarries. Such sites are often characterised by the presence of limestone loving (calcicolous) plants including kidney vetch, burnet saxifrage, great knapweed and many more. The sparse flora of low growing plants and patches of bare soil on ant hills warm up quickly when the sun shines, providing a basking place for butterflies. Ants are essential to butterflies such as Common Blue and Small Blue, as they assist in nurturing the caterpillars. At some stage during their growth - this varies with species - caterpillars will develop ant attracting organs which secrete a honey-like substance. The ants milk the caterpillars for this food, at the same time protecting the grub from predators and parasites. In some butterfly species, the caterpillars will live in the ant's nest and eat their grubs, while in others they may be buried by ants at night, emerging to feed on plants by day. The chrysalis also has a relationship with ants and will attract its body-guards by 'singing' in imitation of noises made by the ants, themselves, as well as with chemical signals. Such a relationship is obviously of benefit to both types of insect, but has its risks, as without ants the caterpillars of 'blues' would find it difficult or impossible to develop to maturity.

Some of the limestone grasslands are Sites of Special Scientific Interest (SSSIs) and some are Warwickshire Wildlife Trust reserves. These are prevented from turning into scrub by either regular cutting or grazing, often by rabbits. However, some scrub is beneficial as shelter and is essential to one of limestone grassland's specialities, the Green Hairstreak. Other important butterfly species to occur in this habitat in Warwickshire are Small Blue, Grizzled and Dingy Skippers and Marbled White.

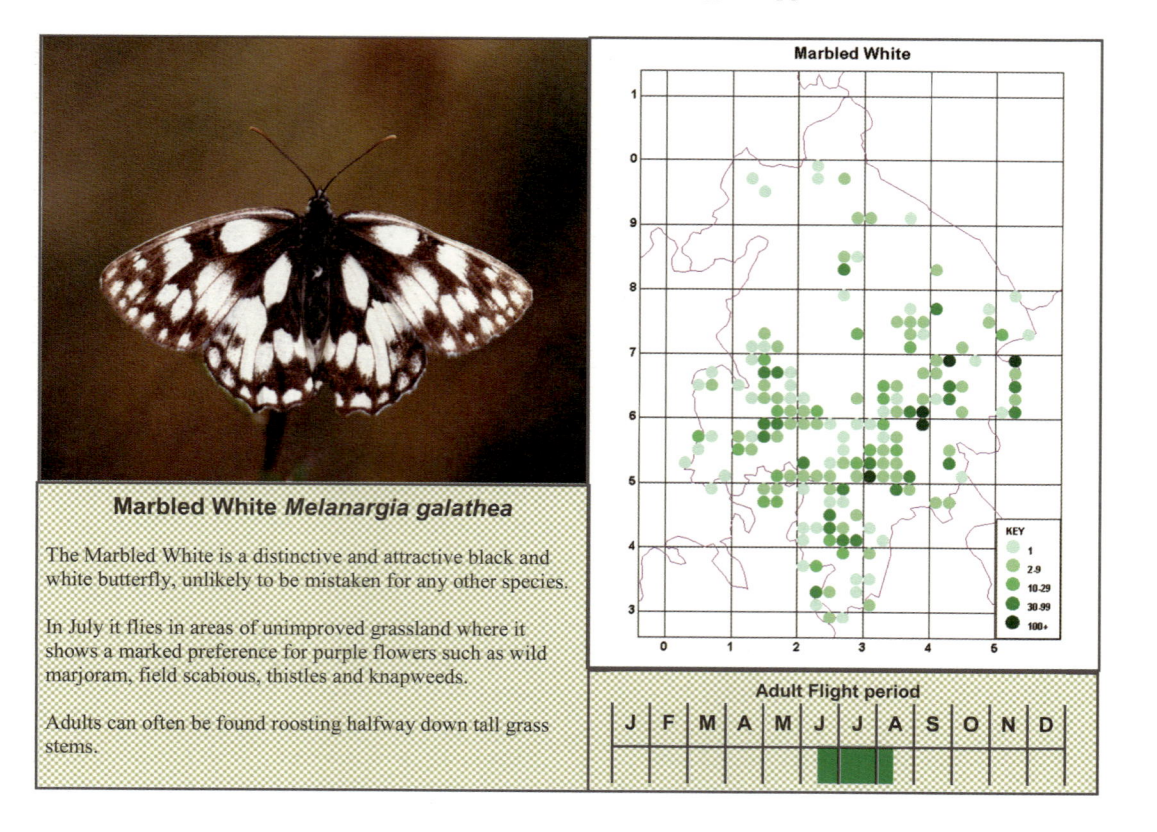

Marbled White *Melanargia galathea*

The Marbled White is a distinctive and attractive black and white butterfly, unlikely to be mistaken for any other species.

In July it flies in areas of unimproved grassland where it shows a marked preference for purple flowers such as wild marjoram, field scabious, thistles and knapweeds.

Adults can often be found roosting halfway down tall grass stems.

Damp Grassland and Meadows

Grassland in floodplains, on badly drained soils and near wetlands will often become flooded in winter. Many of the characteristic plants are caterpillar foodplants such as lady's smock (cuckoo flower) for Orange Tip and Green-veined White, docks for Small Coppers, large bird's foot trefoil for Common Blues, nettles for various nymphalids and grasses for Browns and Skippers. Good nectar plants are also present such as purple loosestrife and hemp agrimony

Tocil wet meadow, Coventry.

The Orange Tip lays a single egg on the underside of the flower buds which appear in spring and the caterpillars eat the developing seeds. The Green-veined White caterpillars eat the leaves so there is no competition between the species. This difference may also explain why the Orange Tip has only one brood and flies in Spring, while the Green-veined White has two main broods and can be seen flying in both Spring and Autumn.

The spindle-shaped egg of the Orange Tip turns a deep orange colour a day or two after being laid. It can be a rewarding pastime revealing the tiny but conspicuous eggs on the underside of the flowers of cuckoo flower or garlic mustard to your astounded friends!

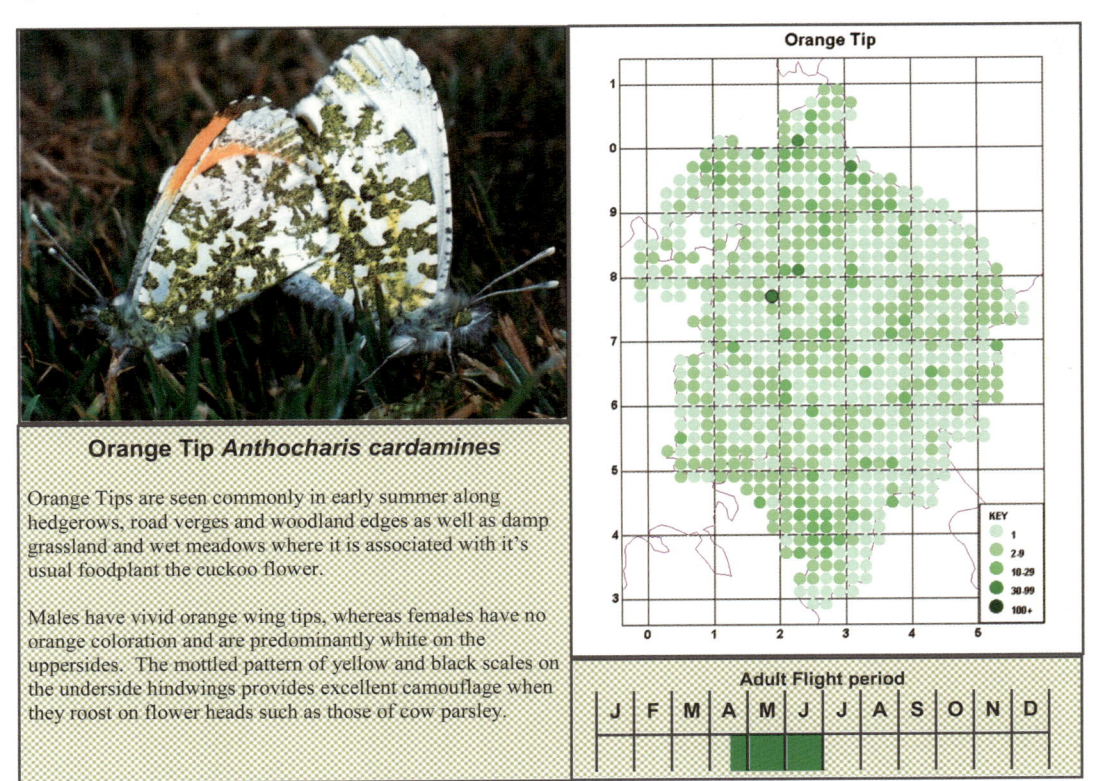

Orange Tip *Anthocharis cardamines*

Orange Tips are seen commonly in early summer along hedgerows, road verges and woodland edges as well as damp grassland and wet meadows where it is associated with it's usual foodplant the cuckoo flower.

Males have vivid orange wing tips, whereas females have no orange coloration and are predominantly white on the uppersides. The mottled pattern of yellow and black scales on the underside hindwings provides excellent camouflage when they roost on flower heads such as those of cow parsley.

Adult Flight period

| J | F | M | A | M | J | J | A | S | O | N | D |

Green-veined White *Pieris napi*

The dusky vein markings on the undersides of the wings of the Green-veined White are variable in colour and make it well camouflaged when it roosts among vegetation.

Recommended Sites:

Harbury Spoilbank Nature Reserve
(SP384598)

An SSSI Owned by Warwickshire Wildlife Trust, this site is an example of a man-made limestone habitat. It is a spoilbank formed when the Birmingham - Oxford railway was excavated in the 1840s. Much limestone grassland is present with many butterfly larval foodplants and nectar plants.

Regular scrub clearance is carried out on the site to increase the abundance of flowers that make the reserve attractive to both human visitors and to butterflies. During the last quarter of the 20th century 29 species of butterfly were recorded here, and although Wood White and Dark Green Fritillary seem now to be extinct on this reserve, it is still possible to see Grizzled and Dingy Skippers, Green Hairstreak, Marbled White, Small Heath and Wall.

Recent plantings of kidney vetch have been made to entice the Small Blue back to the reserve and White-letter Hairstreak was recorded in the 1990s.

Ufton Fields LNR and Country Park
(SP378615)

Ufton Fields is a Local Nature Reserve owned by Warwickshire County Council and managed by Warwickshire Wildlife Trust and is the result of limestone workings in the 1950s.

Also an SSSI, it is a much larger reserve than Harbury Spoilbank and there is a circular way-marked path which passes through a range of habitats, including grassland, woodland and wetland.

The calcareous flora of the grassland areas is similar to that at Harbury Spoilbank and attracts similar butterfly species. Marbled Whites are usually plentiful in the summer and an occasional Small Blue is seen, probably visiting from nearby Harbury.

Stockton Cutting Local Nature Reserve
(SP437651)

Stockton Cutting near Southam is a small reserve formed from a section of abandoned railway cutting with an adjacent spoilbank. It is also owned by Warwickshire County Council and managed by Warwickshire Wildlife Trust and is an SSSI. The underlying limestone and Blue Lias Clay has produced a varied calcareous flora similar to that found at Harbury and Ufton and similar butterfly species are to be found on this reserve, with 31 species having been recorded. Green Hairstreak, Grizzled and Dingy Skippers, and Marbled White are specialities.

The reserve is a very attractive area to visit, especially in the spring and there are paths to guide the visitor, but these are steep in places and can be quite slippery in wet weather, although steps have been cut in the steepest sections.

Meadow Brown *Maniola jurtina*

The Meadow Brown is the most abundant butterfly at many sites. Hundreds can often be seen together, flying low over vegetation. Adults fly even in dull weather when most other species are inactive.

Both sexes have brown wings with a single black eye-spot (normally with a single white 'pupil') surrounded by orange. The female's forewing is more orange and similar to that of the Gatekeeper. The black 'eye-spot' is repeated on the underside, while the brownish hindwing has no white spots.

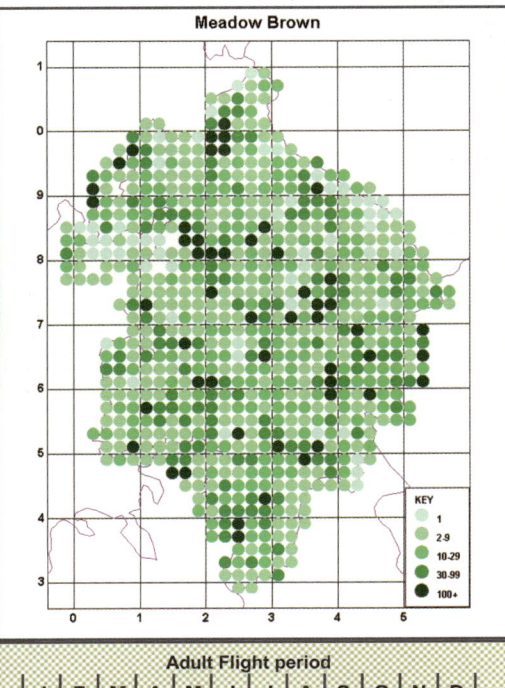

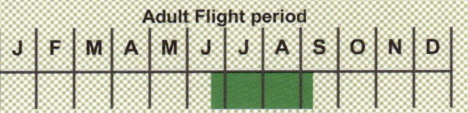

Additional Sites:

Castle Hills, Solihull
(SP177822)

Castle Hills near Solihull has an excellent butterfly population and 26 species have been recorded, with at least 19 breeding on the site.

Of particular note is a small colony of White-letter Hairstreak and Purple Hairstreak is also present. Other residents include Common and Holly Blue, Small Copper and Small Heath. Essex Skipper has been recorded and is possibly breeding on the site.

Two footpaths from Catherine de Barnes Lane cross the site, one leading to Damson Parkway and the other to Old Damson Lane.

Roy Ledbury

Knowle Hill, Kenilworth
(SP298728)

This grassy bank with scrub is a productive site for butterflies on the edge of town. Species include Large, Small and Essex Skipper, Purple Hairstreak, Common Blue, Small Copper, and Ringlet. Marbled White has occurred occasionally.

Welches Meadow LNR, Leamington Spa
(SP325657) **& Eathorpe NR** (SP389687)

The former is an area owned by Warwick District Council that has a mixture of habitats including damp meadows where Orange Tip and Green-veined White occur.

The latter site is owned by Severn Trent Water and managed by Warwickshire Wildlife Trust and although small, is an excellent example of the wetlands that were once widespread in Warwickshire

Small Copper *Lycaena phlaeas*

The Small Copper is the only butterfly with brilliant copper-coloured forewings bearing dark spots and a dark fringe. It is a small butterfly that often perches with it's wings half open.

Males often behave aggressively towards any passing insects, returning to the same spot when the chase is over.

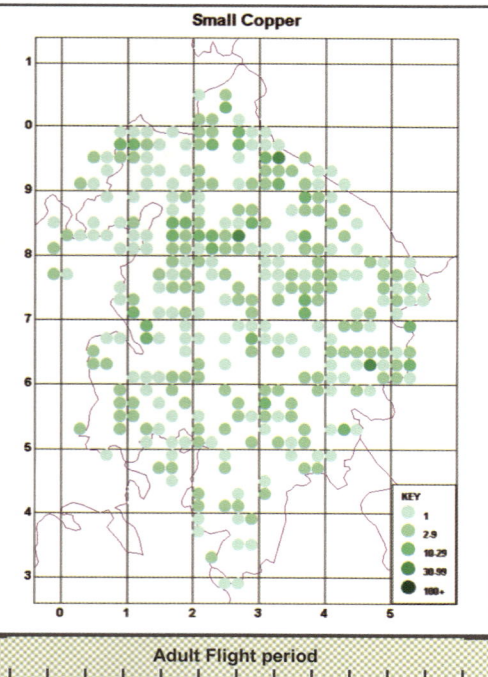

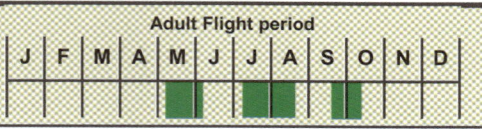

Dark Green Fritillary *Argynnis aglaja*

Although confined to a single site in Warwickshire (the other records being of vagrants), the Dark Green Fritillary is the most widespread of the large fritillaries. It prefers unimproved or limestone grassland.

It is named from the predominantly green colouring of the underside of the hindwings which lack the red-ringed spots of the similar High Brown Fritillary

Adult Flight period

| J | F | M | A | M | J | J | A | S | O | N | D |

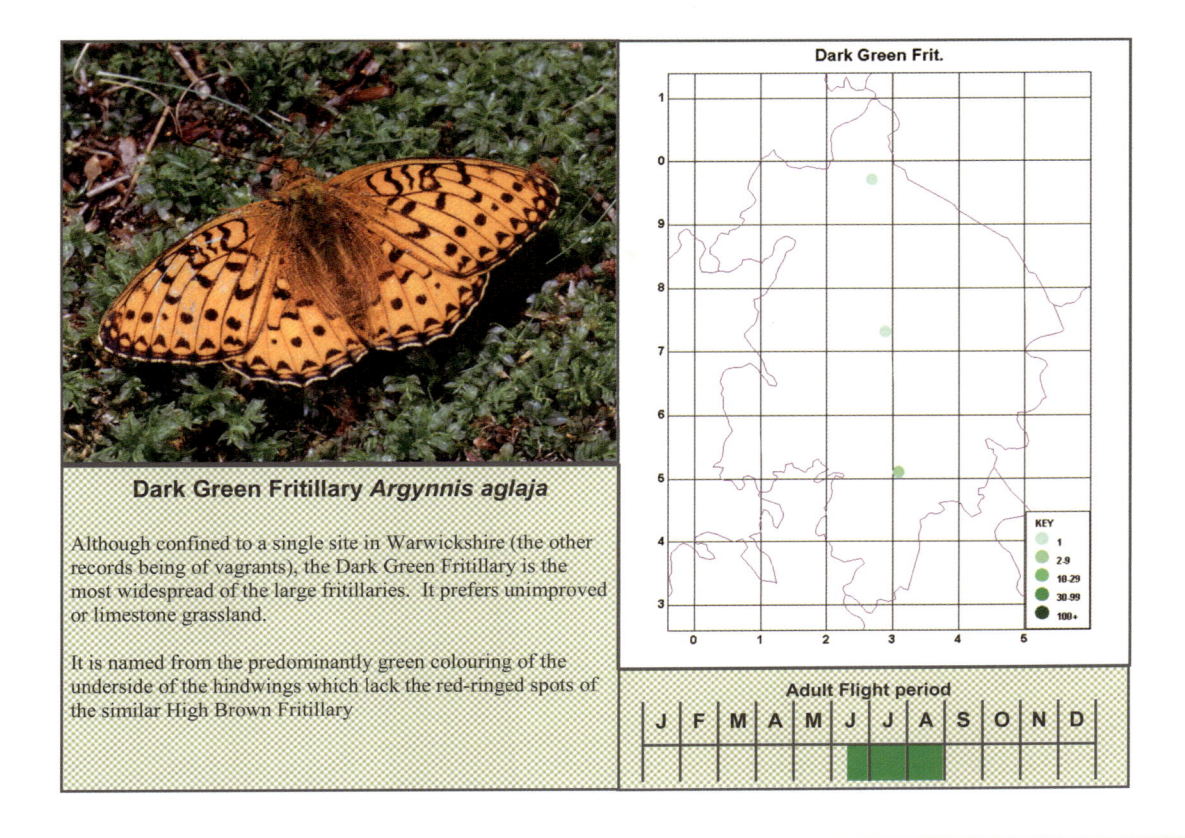

My supreme butterfly day in Warwickshire occurred auspiciously on the 4th July 1976 in what seemed a summer from childhood.

I was leading a guided walk for WARNACT, as it then was, at Oxhouse Farm to reveal the floral and entomological delights of Mary Neal's nature reserve to a sizable group of enthusiasts. The Satyridae were in large numbers: Meadow and Hedge Brown, Ringlet, tatty Speckled Woods and pristine, just emerged Marbled Whites. Small Heaths perched everywhere, wings unusually a quarter parted to cool in the heat, plus Large and Small Skippers (no Essex as yet, though hunted even then). Common Blues were indeed that and glorious despite their frequency. The males and females of most of these species were readily demonstrated, there were so many close together, courting or paired. Green-veined, Small and Large White were all present, their sexual differences more subtle and confusable. Nymphalids added to the busy scene, with home-grown Small Tortoiseshell and Painted Lady from foreign parts. A web of Peacock larvae tackled some nettles, but no adults flew. A diffident Comma or two basked apart from the general bustle. White-letter Hairstreak was searched for on the wych elm and in those days, of course, found. There was even a fresh Brimstone doubtless of local provenance from the reserve's common buckthorn.

The highlight amongst these riches came late, as it should, on a patch of spear thistle near the farmhouse – Dark Green Fritillaries – with maybe as many as ten feeding on the nectar and swooping round the admiring observers between top-ups. And that made 19 species. Wow! We should have recorded Small Copper and Red Admiral, but perhaps we looked at too many flowers.

John Roberts

Identification Comparison: Common Blue and Brown Argus

The identification of Brown Argus is often considered difficult as both sexes superficially resemble the brownest form of the female Common Blue. Common Blue females show much variation in the amount of blue and brown colour present on the upperside of their wings, both within colonies and between regions. 'Brown' females tend to predominate in the more southerly colonies in our region often at the same sites as Brown Argus colonies.

The Common Blue has an extra spot near the body on the underside of the forewing. The Brown Argus lacks this spot in the cell of the forewing.

The Brown Argus has a pair of almost vertical spots on the top edge of the hindwing. The Common Blue has a row of spots that form a clean curve on the underside of the hindwing rather than the displaced twin spots.

Common Blue.

Brown Argus.

I've watched you now a full half hour
Self poised upon that yellow flower,
And little butterfly! Indeed
I know not if you sleep or feed,
What joy awaits you, when the breeze
Has found you out among the trees.

William Wordsworth

MAN-MADE HABITAT

Malpass, Rugby *Keith Warmington*

Hedgerows and Roadside Verges

Whatcote to Brailes Lane, South Warwickshire — Keith Warmington

Driving along the by-roads of Warwickshire it may not be obvious that these can be good butterfly habitats. In spring you may see the odd Brimstone or male Orange Tip patrolling up and down its territorial length of hedgerow, but the summer species such as Meadow Brown and Gatekeeper are all too easily missed. Stop the car though and take a leisurely stroll and you could be amazed at what you will see!

The plants growing on roadside verges will reflect the underlying soil type, although the residues from the limestone brought in originally to construct the road can have an influence on the plants and, hence, the butterfly species

Gatekeeper (Hedge Brown) *Pyronia tithonus*

As its name suggests, this butterfly is often encountered where clumps of flowers grow by gateways and along hedgerows.

Distinguished from the similar Meadow Brown by the small white spots on the underside of the hind wing and the two white 'pupils' on the black 'eye-spot' on each forewing.

KEY: 1, 2-9, 10-29, 30-99, 100+

Adult Flight period: J F M A M J J A S O N D

White-letter Hairstreak *Satyrium w-album*

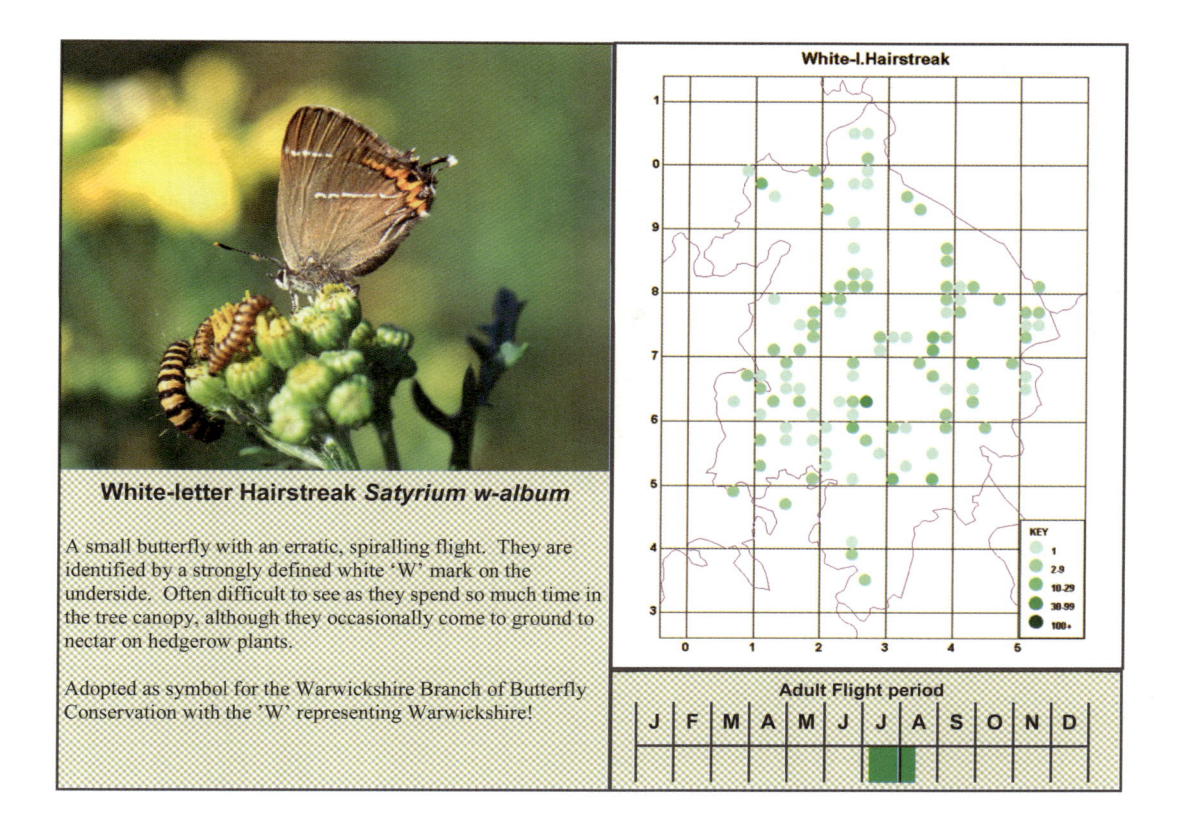

A small butterfly with an erratic, spiralling flight. They are identified by a strongly defined white 'W' mark on the underside. Often difficult to see as they spend so much time in the tree canopy, although they occasionally come to ground to nectar on hedgerow plants.

Adopted as symbol for the Warwickshire Branch of Butterfly Conservation with the 'W' representing Warwickshire!

present. Another important factor is the cutting regime of the verge. If the grass is treated as lawn and cut regularly throughout the season there will be no chance for other plants to flower and set seed. In fact the area will be as barren as a desert for most butterflies and of little interest for the butterfly watcher. Happily, our Warwickshire councils are slowly coming to realise the financial an environmental benefits of cutting only once or twice a year or cutting only a narrow section at the roadside for safety reasons, while leaving the remainder uncut. It is amazing how quickly plants and butterflies return after such a change of management.

Hedges can vary too, from the over trimmed single species to the traditionally managed ancient hedge, with many variations in between. Older hedges usually contain more species of tree and shrub and tend to support a greater variety of wildlife, including butterflies. A hedge containing holly and ivy will almost certainly have a colony of Holly Blue, while oak trees may support Purple Hairstreaks, especially if there are also ash trees close by producing honeydew. In the days before Dutch Elm disease ravaged our elm trees, White-letter Hairstreaks would have been common in hedgerows containing these trees. However it is still possible to find these butterflies in hedges with vigorous and tall elm re-growth.

A roadside verge backed by a hedgerow can

Crimscote verge, South Warwickshire — Keith Warmington

Small Skipper *Thymelicus sylvestris*

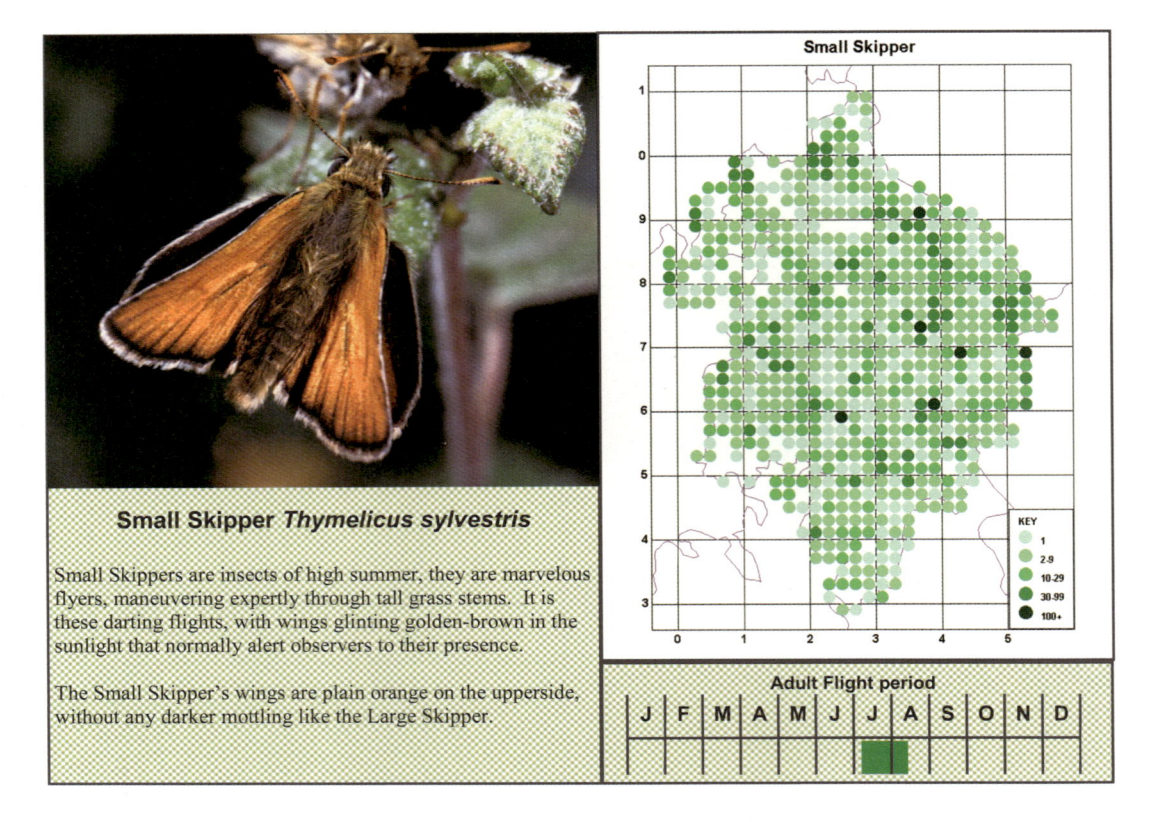

Small Skippers are insects of high summer, they are marvelous flyers, maneuvering expertly through tall grass stems. It is these darting flights, with wings glinting golden-brown in the sunlight that normally alert observers to their presence.

The Small Skipper's wings are plain orange on the upperside, without any darker mottling like the Large Skipper.

make an excellent wildlife corridor, linking larger areas of habitat such as woodland and enabling plants, animals and insects to spread from one site to another. The hedge provides shelter and nectar when bramble or blossoming shrubs such as blackthorn or sallow are present. The adjacent verge can provide both caterpillar foodplants and nectar plants to feed the adults.

However, such corridors will only be of value if managed in a sympathetic manner by minimising the cutting of the grass and hedge to allow a more natural development.

Moving from one area to another along such a corridor can be a long process for some species, but others spread quite rapidly. The Essex Skipper butterfly colonised much of Warwickshire during the 1990s by moving along roadside verges. It is probably no co-incidence that this took place at a time when councils were cutting back on roadside grass cutting, as the Essex Skipper's preferred habitat is long grass in dry, sunny places (although the recent run of warmer summers will have been a factor.) Garlic mustard is a characteristic plant of damp roadside verges and usually grows along the base of hedgerows, especially where a drainage ditch is present. Where garlic mustard is plentiful there is a good chance of finding the Orange Tip which uses this as one of the caterpillar foodplants. It is also a foodplant for the larvae of Green-veined White, another species frequently found flying along hedgerows.

Many roadside verges are too narrow to become permanent breeding areas but wider ones can form mini grasslands supporting species such as Common Blue, Meadow Brown and occasionally Marbled White, as at the flowery Ettington roundabout verge.

As it's English names suggest, the Gatekeeper (also more appropriately known as the Hedge Brown) is often encountered where clumps of flowers grow in gateways and along hedgerows and field edges.

Old hedgerows containing trees can act like mini woodlands and support colonies of woodland species such as the Speckled Wood butterfly.

Recommended Sites:

Glasshouse Lane, Kenilworth
(SP303726 - 306718)

A most enjoyable walk can be taken along Glasshouse Lane in Kenilworth. There are uncut grass verges, old hedges and many mature trees. Gatekeepers, Speckled Wood and Green-veined White abound and Meadow Browns and Ringlets can be seen on the roadside verge, as can Large and Small Skippers. Both Brimstone and Orange Tip patrol the hedge and White-letter Hairstreak are commonly recorded. Mature gardens back onto part of this road, some with buddleias, ensuring that Peacock and Small Tortoiseshell can also be seen.

A429, Ettington
(SP264492)

Another excellent site is the Ettington roundabout roadside verge on the A429. This is a steep man-made limestone grassland habitat containing many typical plants of this habitat type, including centaury, yellow rattle and pyramidal orchid.

On one visit in July Large Skipper, Small Skipper, Meadow Brown, Gatekeeper, Small Heath, Large and Small Whites, Peacock, Common Blue and Marbled White were all recorded.

Ettington roadside verge, South Warwickshire — Keith Warmington

Small Heath *Coenonympha pamphilus*

The Small Heath is an inconspicuous butterfly that flies only in sunshine and rarely settles more than a metre above the ground. It's wings are always kept closed when at rest.

The number of broods and the flight periods are variable and adults may be seen continuously from late April to September on some sites.

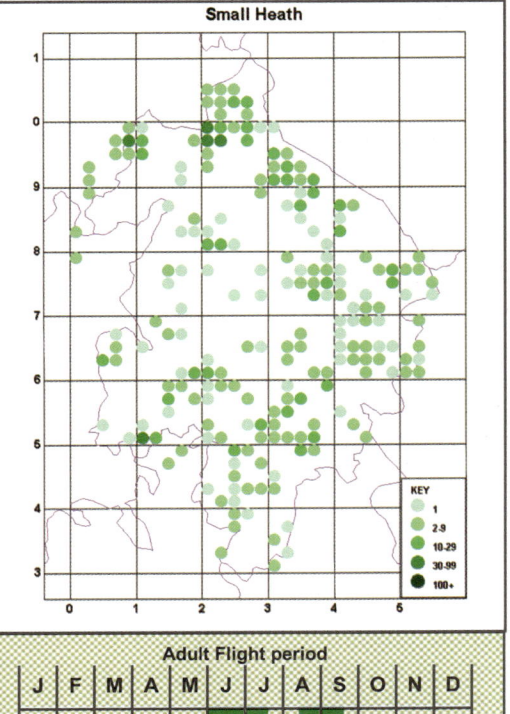

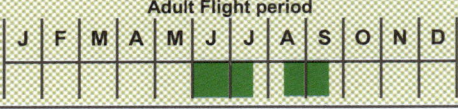

Adult Flight period: J F M A M **J J** A **S** O N D

Clouded Yellow *Colias croceus*

The Clouded Yellow is one of the truly migratory European butterflies and is a regular visitor to the county. Although some of these golden-yellow butterflies are seen every year, the species is famous for occasional mass immigrations and subsequent breeding, which are fondly remembered as 'Clouded Yellow Years'.

A small proportion of females are pale yellow (form *helice*), which can be confused with the rarer Pale and Berger's Clouded Yellows and freshly emerged Large Whites.

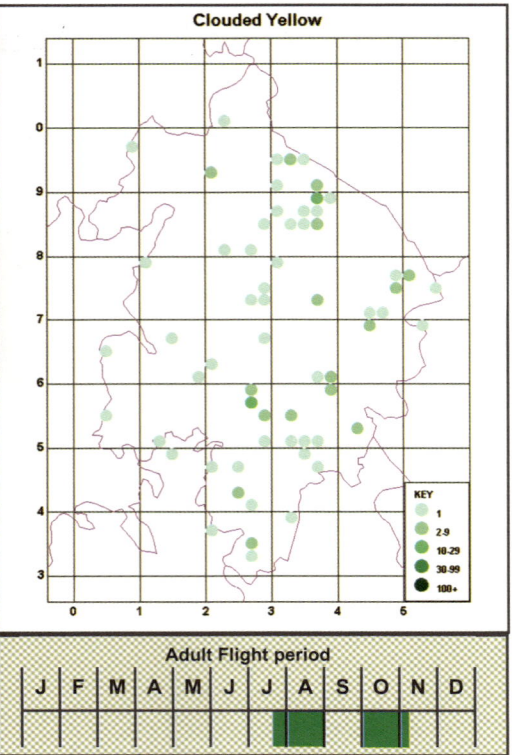

Additional Sites:

Dordon Lane, Dordon
(SP226902)

Large and Small Skippers, White-letter Hairstreak, Purple Hairstreak, Common Blue, Holly Blue, Small, Large and Green-veined whites, Orange Tip, Small Tortoiseshell, Peacock, Gatekeeper, Meadow Brown and Small Heath.

Castle Lane, Shustoke
(SP226902)

Large and Small Skipper, Large and Small White, Small Copper, Common Blue, Gatekeeper and Meadow Brown.

Fulready to Whatcote Lane
(SP294453)

Small Skipper, Brimstone, Orange Tip, Common Blue, Marbled White, Gatekeeper, Meadow Brown, Ringlet.

Crimscote to Newbold Lane
(SP236472)

Small Skipper, Small White, Common Blue, Comma, Gatekeeper, Meadow Brown and 5 Spot Burnet Moth.

**Pailton to Harborough Magna
(M6 Overbridge)**
(SP477805)

Essex Skipper, Gatekeeper, Meadow Brown.

**Paget's Lane, Bubbenhall
(Before Shrubs Lodge)**
(SP373720)

Purple Hairstreak, White-letter Hairstreak.

Field Margins and Headlands

In many instances field margins and headlands are the habitat on one side of the hedge or fence and road verges are the habitat on the other side. Unless the adjacent habitats are vastly different the butterfly species found in both are likely to be similar. The way a field is managed will have a considerable effect on the numbers of butterflies and the species found along its edges.

Butterfly Conservation member Phil Pain regularly visited the fields of two nearby Warwickshire farms in 1997 and counted the butterflies. One was managed organically and one conventionally. He noted 20 species in the organic fields but only 15 in those managed conventionally. A total count of 342 butterflies was made for the organic farm, which was nearly three times as many as the 122 for the conventional farm. The only species which seemed to do as well on both farms were Large and Small Whites.

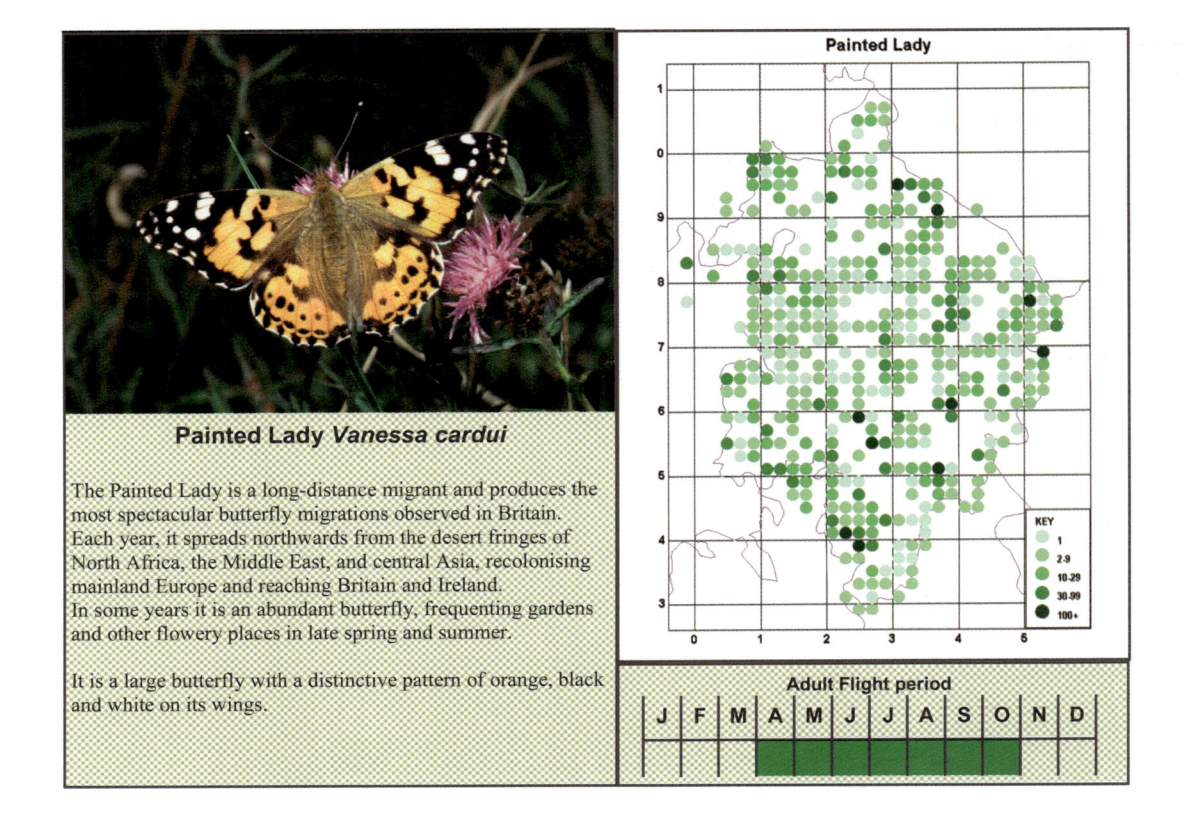

Field margin wildflowers, South Warwickshire — John Roberts

Painted Lady *Vanessa cardui*

The Painted Lady is a long-distance migrant and produces the most spectacular butterfly migrations observed in Britain. Each year, it spreads northwards from the desert fringes of North Africa, the Middle East, and central Asia, recolonising mainland Europe and reaching Britain and Ireland.
In some years it is an abundant butterfly, frequenting gardens and other flowery places in late spring and summer.

It is a large butterfly with a distinctive pattern of orange, black and white on its wings.

Adult Flight period: J F M A M J J A S O N D

Disused Railway Lines

Stockton Old Railway Cutting. John Roberts

A surprising number of disused railway lines criss-cross Warwickshire and Ordnance Survey maps are probably the best tools to help you find them. Railway lines, especially disused ones, act as important wildlife corridors. The type of habitat within the corridor dictates the species best able to make use of it.

When the railway cuttings were first excavated they often exposed nutrient-poor sub-soils which give rise to flower-rich grasslands. These grasslands can support fine grasses and various herbs which are caterpillar foodplants for many grassland species. They also support a rich flora of nectar plants.

Grizzled Skipper *Pyrgus malvae*

The Grizzled Skipper is a rapid flier in the sunshine and it's rapid, buzzing flight can make it difficult to follow. However, it stops regularly either to perch on a prominent twig or to feed on flowers such as bird's-foot-trefoil, bugle or its foodplant, wild strawberry where it can then be readily identified by the black and white checkerboard pattern on it's wings.

At night and in dull weather the Grizzled Skipper rests, often communally, on grass or dead flower heads.

Adult Flight period

J	F	M	A	M	J	J	A	S	O	N	D
				■	■						

KEY: 1, 2-9, 10-29, 30-99, 100+

Green Hairstreak *Callophyrs rubi*

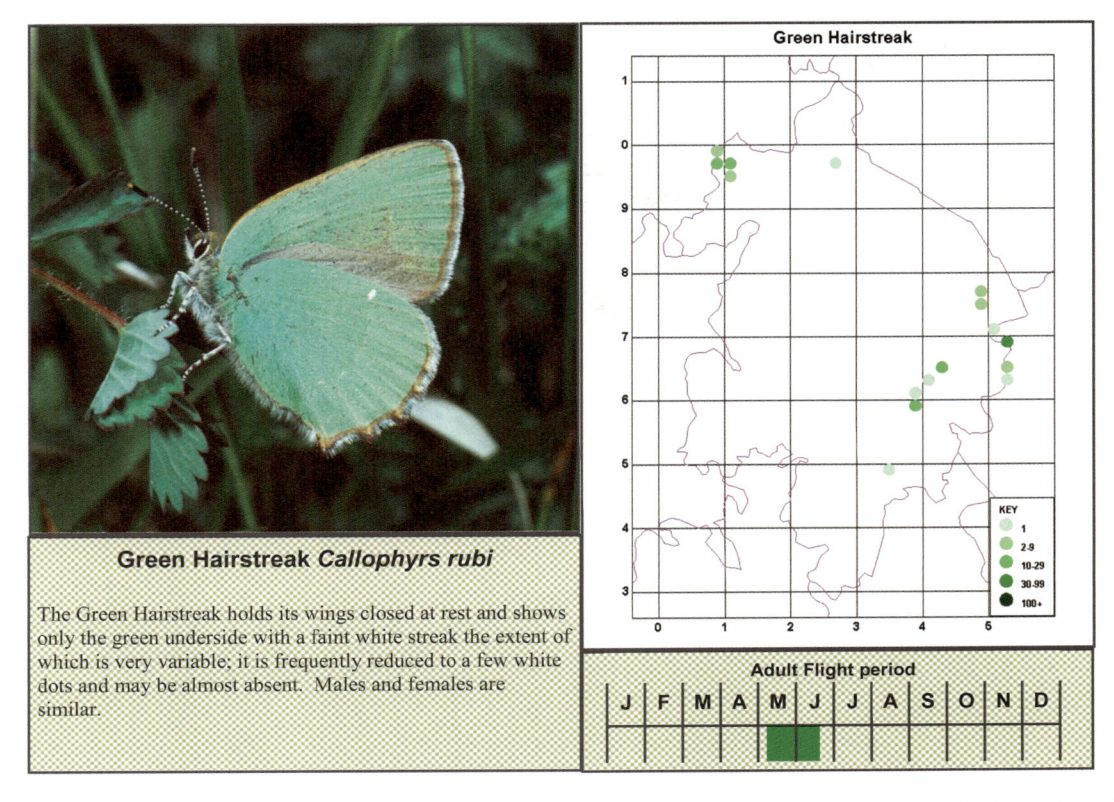

The Green Hairstreak holds its wings closed at rest and shows only the green underside with a faint white streak the extent of which is very variable; it is frequently reduced to a few white dots and may be almost absent. Males and females are similar.

In the 1960's, many of these railways served quarries and collieries and the cuttings and embankments were managed to reduce the effect of accidental fires. The grassland thus preserved was rich in plants and insects. With the demise of the railways and their management, much of the species rich grasslands have been invaded by scrub, gradually at first, but then at an increasing rate following myxamatosis in the rabbit population. Now forty or so years on, many of these lines are now woodland and what little grassland remains has become coarse and species poor. Where nature reserves have been established on some of the old railways, efforts have been made to reintroduce grassland management. This is surprisingly labour intensive and resources are limited and so it is rather a loosing battle. Sites surveyed between the years 1995 and 2000 for the recently published Millennium Atlas of Butterflies are showing a steady loss of grassland species, particularly, Green Hairstreak, Grizzled Skipper and Dingy Skipper and Warwickshire conforms to this pattern. Fortunately not all our butterflies require a grassland habitat, even flowers of some of the scrub species such as bramble and blackthorn provide useful nectar, so it is still worth exploring the old railway lines. However, many of the disused lines are privately owned so permission should be sort before venturing onto such sites.

Rugby Borough Council owns five and a half miles of the former Great Central Railway line and this is perhaps typical of the best of Warwickshire's old lines. The southern half of this line comprises Ashlawn Cutting Nature Reserve which is managed by Warwickshire Wildlife Trust. The northern part which includes Newton Cutting, is classed as a Local Nature Reserve but this currently has no formal arrangement for habitat management. Fortunately the rabbit population here is doing the best it can to control the scrub!

Both Ashlawn and Newton Cuttings have areas with pussy willow and blackthorn, the flowers of which are an excellent source of nectar for emerging hibernators. Look in sheltered sunny spots for Brimstones, Tortoiseshells, Peacocks, and Commas, from the beginning of March. The other important nectar source at this time is the yellow coltsfoot flower, usually found by the

Essex Skipper *Thymelicus lineola*

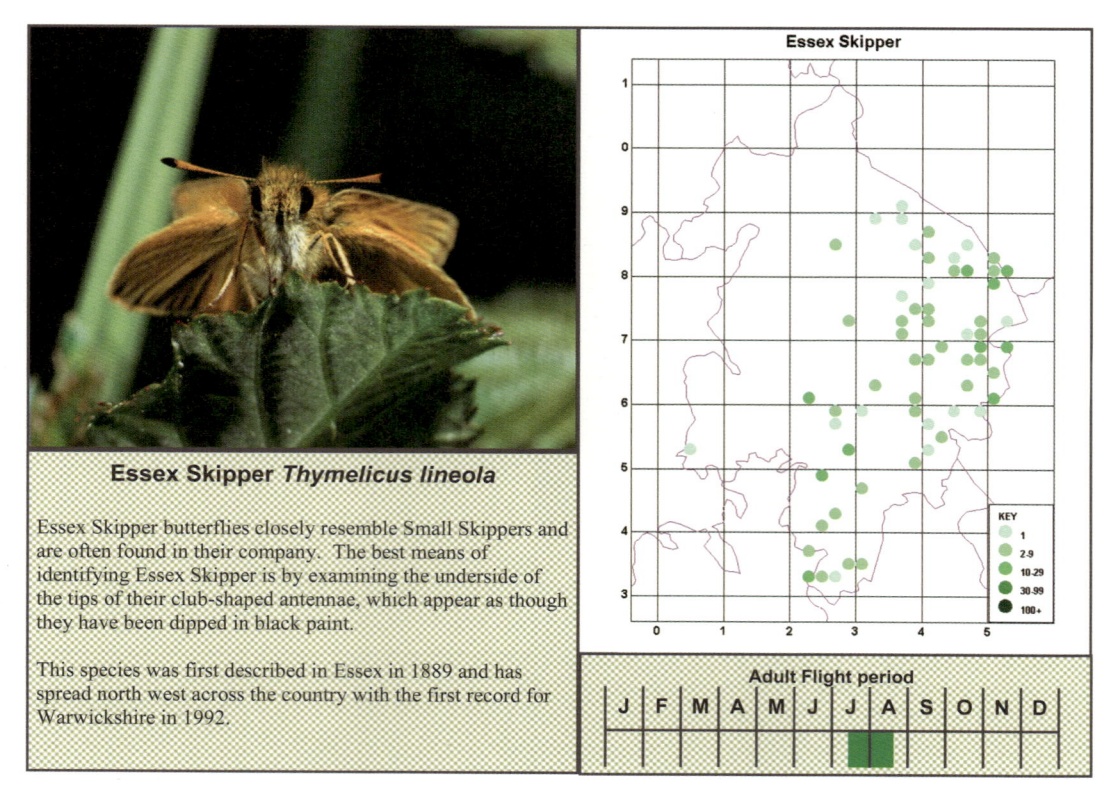

Essex Skipper butterflies closely resemble Small Skippers and are often found in their company. The best means of identifying Essex Skipper is by examining the underside of the tips of their club-shaped antennae, which appear as though they have been dipped in black paint.

This species was first described in Essex in 1889 and has spread north west across the country with the first record for Warwickshire in 1992.

Adult Flight period

| J | F | M | A | M | J | J | A | S | O | N | D |

KEY: 1, 2-9, 10-29, 30-99, 100+

trackside, in clumps on sunny banks. In April, the first Orange Tips take to the wing. The track drainage in cuttings often becomes impeded producing areas of marsh. The flowers of lady's smock may be found here, and even on days when the butterfly is not on the wing, it is worth a search around the flower buds for it's orange eggs.

The Speckled Wood butterfly was rare in Rugby prior to 1987 but in September of that year two were seen in Ashlawn Cutting. By 1989 there were more than 70 sightings in Rugby but it was still not being recorded to the north of the town. In May 1990, three were seen in Newton Cutting and within a couple of years they were common in the cuttings and indeed in most of the gardens in Rugby. The cutting's natural progression from grassland to scrub seems to have provided a corridor that helped this to happen. However, as the shade loving Speckled Wood increased in numbers, grassland species such as Common Blue, Small Copper, and Small Heath decreased.

The Large Skipper reach a peak in June, while the more prolific Small Skipper peaks in July.

Now the grasses are approaching their tallest and wild flowers such as knapweed, thistles and ragwort are at their best.

Newton Cutting, Rugby — Keith Warmington

Goldicote Cutting, Nr. Stratford — John Roberts

Although Dutch Elm disease may have robbed us of many magnificent trees, re-growth from elm rootstock occurs widely. As a consequence White-letter Hairstreak can still be found on the banks of railway cuttings such as Goldicote Cutting just outside Stratford upon Avon and at the Ashlawn Cutting in Rugby. A search for the adult butterfly on sunny July evenings can still be fruitful in spite of the increased elm dieback due to new outbreaks of the disease.

Large Skipper *Ochlodes venata*

The Large Skipper is the most conspicuous of the 'orange' Skippers. The males are most often found perching in a prominent, sunny position, usually on a large leaf at the boundary between taller and shorter vegetation, where they are ready to dart out and attack passing males or to vigorously court passing females.

The presence of a faint chequered pattern on both sides of the wings distinguish this species from the similar Small and Essex Skippers.

KEY
1
2-9
10-29
30-99
100+

Adult Flight period
| J | F | M | A | M | J | J | A | S | O | N | D |

Recommended Sites:

Ashlawn Railway Cutting, Rugby
(SP517732)

Ashlawn Railway Cutting Nature Reserve consists of two very steep, well drained cutting sides which rise sharply from the old track bed, running in a north to south direction. Access is from Ashlawn Road, Rugby by the bridge. The habitat is predominantly scrub with some open grassy banks that are good for butterflies. More importantly, it is the only known site for the day-flying Forester Moth in Warwickshire. This attractive green moth can be seen on the wing from late May to July and prefers the open, flowery, west slopes of the cutting. Butterflies here include Brimstone, Common Blue, Marbled White and Ringlet.

David Brown

Henley Sidings, Henley in Arden
(SP147669)

Henley Sidings in Henley in Arden is a disused railway sidings owned by Warwickshire Wildlife Trust. The reserve is predominantly calcareous grassland on infertile soil with areas of scrub, neutral grassland and a small pond. The reserve's greatest treasure is a colony of Marbled Whites, but there is also a good colony of Common Blues. Over 20 species of butterfly have been recorded, including Small Heath and a single Clouded Yellow.

Please note that Henley Sidings has no car park and visitors are asked to park at the north (Birmingham) end of Henley near Johnson Place and walk a few yards towards Birmingham before taking the footpath to the left and then the lane towards Henley Golf Club. Just before the Golf Club turn right towards Park Farm and the reserve is on the left just before the farmyard.

Ted Read

Weddington Old Railway Line, Nuneaton
(SP359943)

The Weddington Country Walk, accessed from Weddington Road, Nuneaton, follows the old railway line and supports a variety of habitats. Large numbers of Speckled Wood and Gatekeeper frequent the more shaded stretches and Common Blue, Small Copper and Small Heath can be found in the grassy areas.

Look out for the Wall butterfly, which is becoming scarce in Warwickshire. It is present here in small numbers where bare patches of soil are to be found on the banks.

Keith Warmington

Ashlawn Railway Cutting, Rugby. — Daniel L. Warwood

Additional Sites:

The Greenway, Stratford-on-Avon
(SP196540)

This public path follows a five mile section of the old Stratford to Honeybourne railway line that was closed in 1976. Species include Marbled White, Purple Hairstreak, Common Blue, Ringlet and Small Heath.

Newton Railway Cutting, Rugby
(SP529785)

The disused railway cutting is accessed from the picnic site north of Newton village on the outskirts of Rugby. Species include Large and Small Skipper, Orange Tip, Holly Blue, Common Blue, Small Copper, Gatekeeper, Meadow Brown, Wall and Small Heath.

Newton Cutting, Rugby. — Keith Warmington

It isn't just butterflies that catch my eye on the grassy railway banks, the appearance of some of the more unusual wild flowers form part of my annual calendar. A particular favourite is a member of the pea family called Grass Vetchling, As its name suggests its leaves are almost impossible to differentiate from the grasses, but for a few days only in June it has the most beautiful crimson red long stemmed flowers like a miniature pea which in certain places in Ashlawn and Newton cuttings you will find dotted amongst the grasses.

In July, when the grasses are approaching their tallest and wild flowers such as knapweed are at their best, the butterflies can be found in greater numbers. One year I spent a happy half hour or so on a sunny day photographing several Small Skippers nectaring on spectacularly large clump of wild basil. I was totally absorbed and this to me is what butterfly watching is all about.

Phil Parr

Gardens

Gardens are possibly the most widespread and diverse butterfly habitat in the county. Whether large or small, sunny or shady, windswept or sheltered, rural, suburban or urban, gardens are important to Warwickshire's butterflies as sources of nectar and sometimes, larval foodplants. At some time or another all Warwickshire's butterfly species have visited a garden.

The garden habitat differs significantly from almost all others included in this book in that it is totally man-made and can experience quite drastic changes from one year to the next. An important factor for the butterfly watcher is that the garden is, quite literally, there on your doorstep thus giving ample opportunities to observe butterfly visitors.

Peacock *Inachis io*

This is an unmistakable butterfly that is commonly seen on garden buddleia. The large 'eye-spots' on the wings resemble those on the tail feathers of the Peacock bird. This pattern has evolved to startle and confuse predators.

When not congregating in large numbers at good nectar sources, those Peacocks on the wing later in the year spend time prospecting for suitable hibernation sites such as unheated sheds and garages where they will then spend the winter.

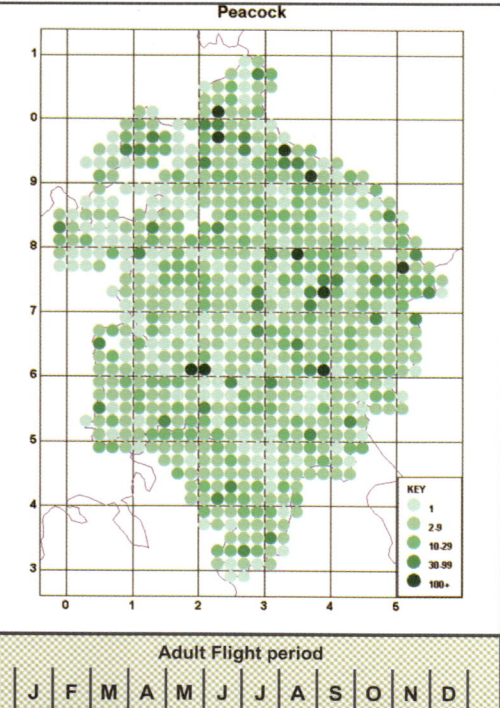

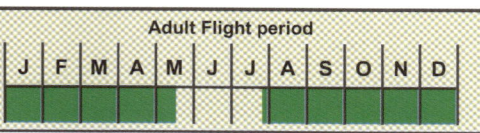

Small White *Pieris rapae*

The Small White is less boldly marked and smaller than it's relative, the Large White. The dark wing-tip is always paler and does not extend down the wing edge. The underside of the hindwing is pale yellow with a dusting of grey.

Adult butterflies are often attracted to white flowers where they feed and on which they are well camouflaged when roosting.

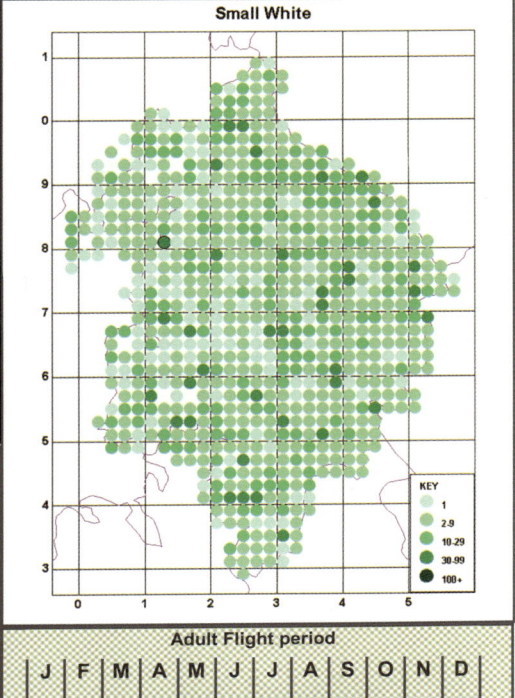

Small White distribution map

KEY: 1 / 2-9 / 10-29 / 30-99 / 100+

Adult Flight period

| J | F | M | A | M | J | J | A | S | O | N | D |

Warwickshire's Garden Butterfly Survey

Warwickshire forms part of the National Butterfly Conservation garden butterfly survey, which determines the percentage of gardens visited each year by each butterfly species.

This survey has shown that there are 22 species which regularly visit gardens and these can be divided into three categories of butterfly visitors: widespread, less common and rare.

****

The average percentage of Warwickshire gardens visited each year from 1995 - 2000 by the five Widespread butterflies are:

Peacock	97%
Small Tortoiseshell	94%
Large White	93%
Small White	90%
Red Admiral	90%

There are 10 Less Common species and the following percentage of gardens were visited in Warwickshire by these butterflies:

Green-veined White	80%
Orange-tip	78%
Brimstone	74%
Comma	74%
Meadow Brown	73%
Gatekeeper	70%
Speckled Wood	66%
Holly Blue	62%
Painted Lady	57%
Common Blue	37%

There are 7 Rarer butterflies that have visited:

Small Skipper	43%
Small Copper	40%
Large Skipper	37%
Ringlet	30%
Marbled White	9%
Small Heath	9%
Wall	5%

What we grow in our gardens will to some extent influence the butterfly species we see. For example, Helen Newell's garden in Kenilworth (described below) is one of those in which provision for wildlife takes precedence over conventional gardening. Margaret Vickery's garden nearby (described on page 43), on the other hand, is a more conventional garden that has been carefully and selectively planted with the nectar rich species that butterflies prefer. Even the dullest gardens can expect visitations by prospecting butterflies, even if they fail to stay long.

I grow both nectar plants and caterpillar foodplants in my garden in Kenilworth, which totals about 200 sq. m. In the 9 years I've been here, 23 species of butterfly have visited, of which at least 13 species have laid eggs. It is difficult to be sure how many of these eggs are successful in producing butterflies, though I've found caterpillars of 8 species.

Speckled Woods will lay on blades of Yorkshire fog grass, within 5m of the house in full shade. Gatekeepers prefer the fine-leaved grass on the sunny side of the base of my buddleia, and their numbers have increased dramatically since my alterations to the garden. The profusion of native grasses allowed to grow tall has also favoured Meadow Browns, Ringlets and the skippers.

Garlic mustard in the garden has been used by Orange Tip and Green-veined White, and stinging nettles by Small Tortoiseshell and Red Admiral. I have had some success with birds-foot trefoil for the Common Blue, sorrel for the Small Copper, the shrub buckthorn for Brimstone and a young wych elm for Commas positioned away from the house at the end of the garden). I avoid encouraging the cabbage whites to breed in the interests of neighbour relations!

The ivy which has been allowed to climb upwards and is beginning to flower, will perhaps tempt Holly Blues to lay soon....

Helen Newell

Large White *Pieris brassicae*

Common in Warwickshire.

The Large White has more extensive black wing tips than other Whites, with butterflies of the second brood more heavily marked than the first. Males lack the black spots and streak on the upperside of the forewings.

It is not always welcomed in gardens and fields because of the voracious appetite of its caterpillars.

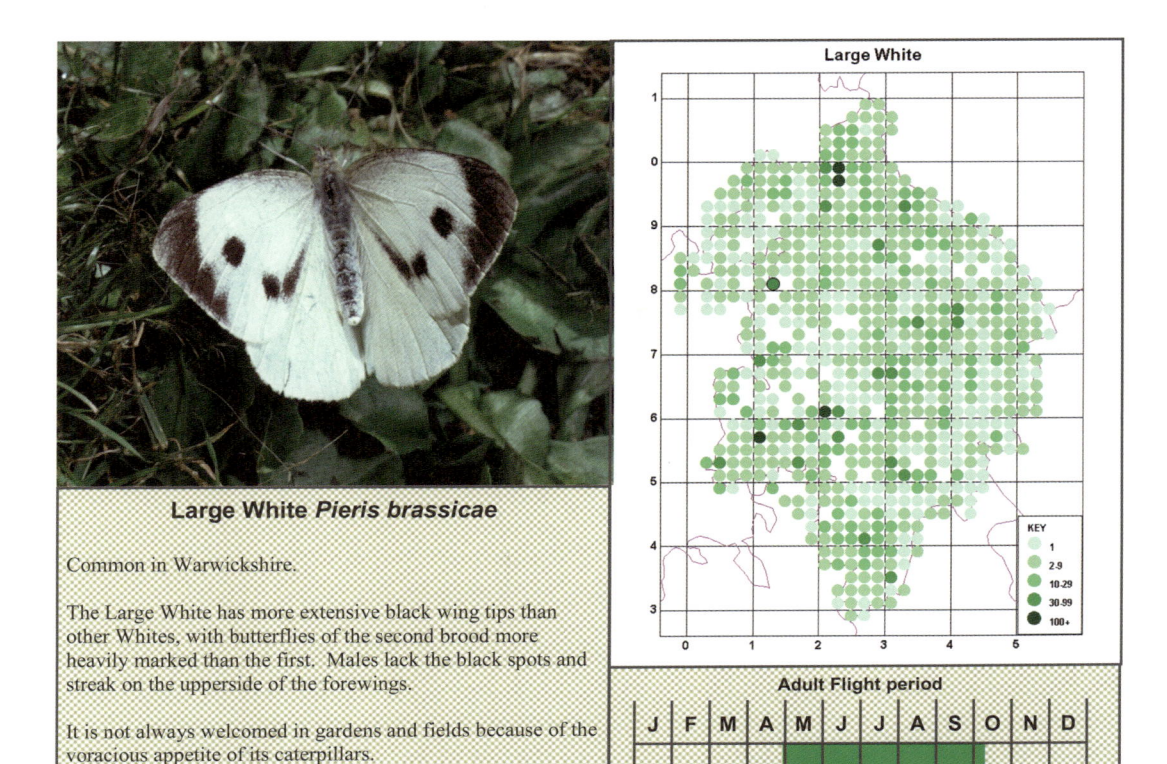

Although I grow a few larval foodplants, including flowering ivy which is used every year by Holly Blues, my garden is mainly devoted to nectar plants.

Like most other butterfly gardeners I have several buddleia bushes, which attract most butterfly species when in flower. Marjoram is popular with Gatekeepers and Meadow Browns, while the yellow common fleabane is a magnet for Small Coppers and Common Blues. In the spring sweet rocket is both a nectar and larval foodplant for Orange Tips. I've found that Bowles purple wallflower and Verbena bonariensis attract a number of species. The long, upright stems of this verbena make excellent perching posts for male Commas and Large Skippers.

At the beginning of the garden butterfly survey in 1990, Speckled Woods seldom visited my gardens and when they did it would be only to bask in the sun. Now, I get many visits and they nectar on marjoram, just like Gatekeepers. There are still ample trees around exuding honeydew so I wonder if this is something they have learned to feed on, in the same way that robins and dunnocks now feed on peanuts in gardens?

Probably, my greatest thrill was a visit by a Silver-washed Fritillary, but there have also been one-off visits by Brown Argus, Essex Skipper and Purple Hairstreak and visits by several Marbled Whites over the years.

Margaret Vickery

Parks and Urban Habitats

Urban habitats are often of great value to butterflies and moths. It is also in such places that people can most easily come into contact with butterflies away from their gardens. Species such as Brimstone, Meadow Brown and Common Blue have been recorded in the centre of Coventry, as well as the more common urban butterflies such as Peacock and Small Tortoiseshell. With intensive farming practices making so many rural areas inhospitable for insects, open spaces in towns and villages can be important breeding areas for a variety of species.

Parks vary greatly in character; some are butterfly friendly, others are not. Some are little more than large areas of mown grass, but flower-rich grassland, woodland or scrub can be present and even specifically managed for wildlife. Some others have a diverse cultivated plant community which is comparable to a large Garden and can result in an abundance of nectar producing plants.

Jephson Gardens in Leamington Spa is an example of the latter and also has a specific butterfly garden (see page 46). Also in Leamington Spa, the Leam Fields, beside the River Leam are good butterfly habitat for grassland species, while Shrublands Recreational Fields, a recently sown area off Europa Way is developing nicely. Whitnash Brook off the Radford Road has Marbled Whites at the southern end as well as 15 other species.

Several parks in Warwick have good butterfly populations. Seventeen species have been recorded at Kingfisher Pools in St Nicholas Park including Common Blue, Small Copper, Small and Large Skippers and Ringlet.

Northern Enclosure, off the Birmingham Road, a developing plantation woodland on a ridge and furrow field, has an excellent population of 20 species including all the above plus Marbled White, Brown Argus and Small Heath. Another good site is St Mary's Land, the central grassland area of Warwick Racecourse, which beside recording a variety of butterflies has a population

Jepson Gardens, Leamington Spa — John Roberts

Red Admiral *Vanessa atalanta*

The striking black, red and white pattern of the Red Admiral is unmistakable. This butterfly is found almost anywhere, particularly gardens, old orchards and uncultivated land where there is an abundance of flowers, nettles and rotting fruit.

This strong flying species migrates to northern Europe each spring from North Africa and continental Europe. In recent years numbers have increased and there have been several reports of successful overwintering.

of the Chimney Sweeper moth. Saltisford Common is also a productive site for butterflies.

Abbey Fields in Kenilworth, although regularly cut throughout the summer, can boast at least 14 species. Attempts were made to leave uncut areas but were frustrated by some park users who complained that it looked untidy.

Warwick District Council's policy on wildlife is to promote the best use of urban open space and promote the best practice in conservation management, developing Local Nature Reserves (LNRs) where possible and green corridors to link habitats. This District Council has designated eight LNRs. Welshes Meadow and Leam Valley in Leamington Spa are both good butterfly habitats and are breeding areas for the now uncommon Small Heath. Marbled White and Brown Argus occur at Welshes Meadow, while Leam Valley has a Purple Hairstreak colony.

Kenilworth has four LNRs: Crackley Wood and Kenilworth Common, which are woodlands and Knowle Hill and Parliament Piece, which are mainly grassland. They all have good populations of butterflies; with woodland ride species, including Purple Hairstreak, Brimstone, Comma, Large and Small Skippers, Small Copper, Ringlet and Holly Blue breeding in the first two. Marbled White occurs sporadically on Knowle Hill, which also has a colonies of Small Copper and Purple Hairstreak. Parliament Piece is a haven for grassland species, including Large and Small Skippers and Meadow Brown. Hundreds of Meadow Browns can be seen flying over the meadow in a good year.

The city of Coventry has some 50 Sites of Importance for Nature Conservation and was the first of our local authorities to complete its comprehensive designation of these sites.

The towns of Nuneaton, Bedworth and Rugby all have parks within easy reach of their centres and species such as Brimstone, Holly Blue, Peacock and Speckled Wood are often seen here.

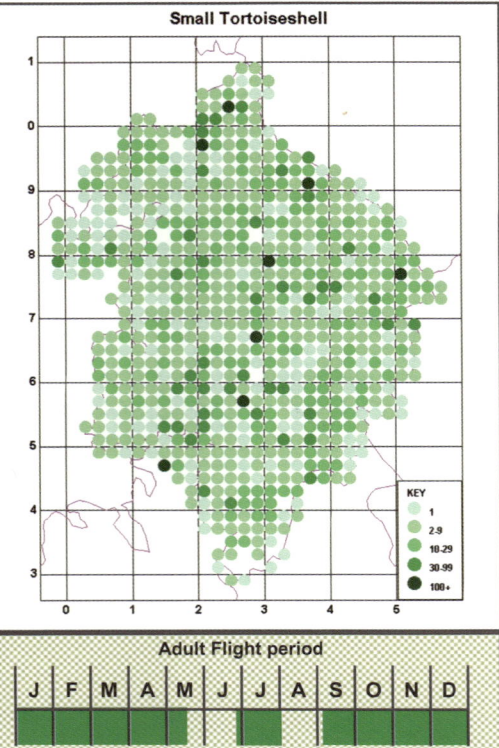

Small Tortoiseshell *Aglais urticae*

The Small Tortoiseshell is perhaps one of the best known butterflies in Britain. The strikingly attractive patterning and its high frequency in urban areas have made it very familiar. It is often one of the first butterflies to be seen in spring and in the autumn it often visits gardens in large numbers, particularly liking the flowers of sedum and michaelmas daisies.

Adult Flight period

J	F	M	A	M	J	J	A	S	O	N	D
■	■	■	■	■		■	■	■	■	■	■

KEY: 1, 2-9, 10-29, 30-99, 100+

Recommended Sites:

Jephson Gardens Butterfly Garden, Leamington Spa
(SP321657)

The butterfly nectar garden is situated adjacent to the toilet block and is accessible from the Newbold Terrace entrance.

Plants include a mix of ornamental shrubs, herbaceous perennials and wild flowers to provide nectar throughout the year. Plants present include buddleia, ice plant, Munsted dwarf lavender, marjoram and field scabious. Climbers on the building are also butterfly friendly with *Escallonia biffida*, providing nectar in autumn for Red Admirals and Small Tortoiseshells.

Butterflies recorded include Holly Blue, Orange Tip, Large Skipper, Speckled Wood, Meadow Brown, Gatekeeper, Brimstone, Comma, Red Admiral, Peacock, Small Tortoiseshell and Large, Small and Green-veined Whites.

Jon Holmes

Lake View Park, Coventry
(SP315795)

Lake View Park in Coventry consists of about 40 acres of grassland containing trees and shrubs with an adjacent area of about 30 acres of mostly abandoned allotments.

Twenty species of butterfly have been recorded: Large and Small Skippers, Brimstone, Orange Tip, Large, Small and Green-veined Whites, Small Copper, Common Blue, Holly Blue, Red Admiral, Small Tortoiseshell, Comma, Peacock, Ringlet, Speckled Wood, Gatekeeper, Meadow Brown, Small Heath and Wall.

The moth population includes Garden Carpet, Cinnabar, Large Yellow Underwing and Red Underwing, Cream Wave, Garden Tiger and Elephant, Eyed and Lime Hawk Moths.

The park is best accessed from Lake View Avenue and Four Pounds Avenue or Grayswood Avenue.

Dave Cole

Stratford Butterfly Farm, Stratford upon Avon
(SP204546)

The British Butterfly garden at Stratford Butterfly Farm is planted either side of the entrance path, so that visitors walk through a temperate butterfly display on their way to the tropics. Well over 20 different species of butterfly have been recorded in the garden over the years, with each year getting into at least the high teens of species numbers.

Many of the best butterfly attracting plants are planted in large blocks for maximum effect. There are nearly 70 metres of buddleia hedge.

During the Painted Lady invasion of 1996 there were at least 100 butterflies per metre. There is a new type of buddleia from China that flowers in September much later than the common ones. In 2000 it attracted many migrants, including Clouded Yellows, when there were few other plants in flower. Other plants include, sedum, scabious, aster, oregano, thyme, valerian, hemp agrimony, lavender, verbena, eupatorium, echinops and aubretia.

Wet summers are not usually very good for the garden, as a lot of nectar seems to be washed out of the buddleia. In dry summers however, as it is watered, the garden seems to pull in many of the butterflies from the surrounding countryside. These include Marbled Whites from an old railway cutting nearly a mile away. Common Blues used to stray from a nearby bit of waste ground before it was built on.

Food plants are also included in the garden. There is an oak tree, and a disease resistant elm "Sapporo Gold" though no hairstreaks have been recorded yet. There is a holly and ivy hedge and Brimstones and Holly Blues are frequent visitors. There is a 'beetle bank' of rough grass and weeds where some of the Browns have been recorded breeding. A wildlife pond for breeding dragonflies, frogs and newts is also a feature of the garden.

Moths have not been forgotten. There is an area planted with honeysuckle, evening primrose and night scented stock. On a recent National Moth Night, however, only half a dozen small brown specimens were captured!

Two rather tantalising records exist. A Camberwell Beauty was captured in the garden in early January 1996 after the mass invasion of August 1995. However as the Butterfly Farm had had some Camberwell Beauties the previous May, the record could not go forward as a definite wild butterfly. The other record was of a large Fritillary in 1997, the year that Dark Green Fritillaries were found at Oxhouse Farm. This particular fritillary was flying too fast for a proper look but a Silver-Washed was seen across the river in the churchyard around the same time.

The Butterfly Garden is difficult to keep looking very attractive throughout the year, but at its height in late summer, with all of the hibernating nymphalids fuelling up on the abundant nectar, any winter scruffiness is soon forgiven.

Richard Lamb

Additional Sites:

Middleton Hall, Middleton
(SP192981)

Walled garden with old fashioned herbaceous plants and extensive grounds. Species include Purple Hairstreak, Common Blue, Holly Blue and Wall.

Purple Hairstreak was first identified as a species by Rev. John Ray who lived at Middleton Hall. His contemporary Petiver, named it 'Mr Ray's Purple Streak.'

Ryton Organic Gardens, Ryton on Dunsmore
(SP400746)

Herbaceous, Herb and Bee gardens with wildlife areas. Species include Small and Essex Skipper, Brimstone, Purple Hairstreak, Small Copper and Small Heath.

The National Herb Centre, Warmington
(SP411471)

Herb gardens with nature walk attracting many garden butterfly species.

Churchyards

Churchyards, cemeteries, crematoria and Gardens of Remembrance can become havens for a great variety of wild animals and plants, depending on their geographical situation, whether urban or rural and their management practices. In certain parts of towns and cities, churchyards may be the last remaining open space of any size and they can serve a similar function in areas of intensive farmland.

Although essentially a man-made habitat, having been disturbed perhaps more than once by the digging of graves, churchyards have usually been carved out of meadowland or ancient pastures. The soil between the graves may have remained undisturbed for many years. Some may have been sheep grazed in the distant past which prevented coarse grasses from spreading and choking out the wildflowers. In recent years mowing will have taken the place of grazing animals but the original flora may still remain in the form of unimproved grassland. At some sites areas left uncut until late in the year will resemble summer hay meadows. Attractive grasses and many tall herbaceous plants are allowed to flower and the latter can become valuable nectar sources. Paths mowed through and around such areas help to give the churchyard the appearance of being cared for provided the parishioners are not too sensitive to unmown grass!

Most churchyards will contain a variety of habitats. As well as the grassland there may be woodland, old hedgerows, scrub, brambles, nettlebeds and the church itself. It is this variety of habitats that provide for all the stages of the life cycle of butterflies. Suitable plants, shrubs and trees are used for egg laying, caterpillar feeding and as a source of nectar. Shelter is often provided by the walled garden effect of churchyards and the heat retaining church walls

Alveston Churchyard, Nr Stratford-on-Avon

Keith Warmington

Speckled Wood *Pararge aegeria*

The aptly named Speckled Wood is most often seen basking with wings half open on vegetation in partially shaded woodland with dappled sunlight. Unlike most butterflies it is not a lover of open sunny places and is rarely seen feeding on flowers, preferring to feed on honey-dew produced by aphids.

The male Speckled Wood is fiercely territorial and attacks any rival males that fly into his domain.

Butterflies of the first brood have larger cream spots.

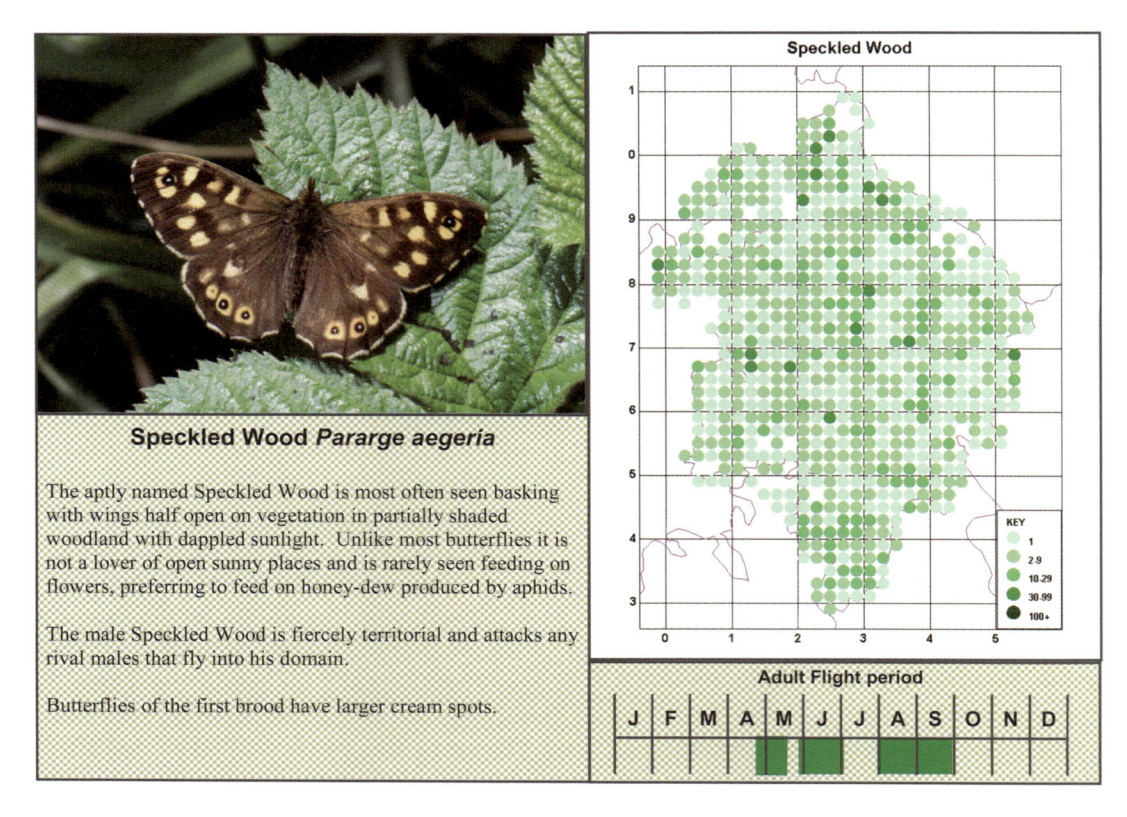

and gravestones provide warm pockets for butterflies. The evergreens commonly associated with churchyards such as yew, holly and ivy provide overwintering roost sites and the ivy flowers make a useful autumn nectar source. Potentially, a large number of butterfly species may be associated with churchyards and a Warwickshire survey concluded that 21 species could easily be found!

The most typical butterfly of English churchyards is the Holly Blue. The first brood of this species flies in early spring and from mid April the butterfly lays her eggs on the unopened flower buds of holly. The caterpillars feed on the immature contents of the holly berries if deposited on a female tree or on young and tender terminal leaves of male holly trees. The second brood emerges in July when there are no holly flowers on which to deposit their eggs and so lay their eggs on unopened flowers of ivy. This practice of alternating foodplant from one brood to another is unique amongst British butterflies.

The timing of the grass cutting in the churchyard is critical for attracting species such as Meadow Brown, Marbled White and Large and Small Skipper. These all prefer a late cut. On the other hand, Small Heath prefers the short grass such as found on paths and lawns.

The perimeter of the churchyard often emulates woodland edge habitat and can attract Speckled Wood and Gatekeeper. Brimstone will roost amongst ivy clad walls and tree trunks. Nettle or bramble patches are a bonus for Small Tortoiseshell, Comma, Peacock and Red Admiral.

In an age where natural habitats in Britain are increasingly lost to development of one kind or another, in a changing countryside such as ours, 10,000 hectares of churchyards must have a considerable value in conserving our native plants and animals.

Recommended Sites:

Oldberrow Churchyard
(SP121660)

Oldberrow Church, close to Henley in Arden, has a small churchyard with a most remarkable diversity of wildflowers, many of which are uncommon in Warwickshire.

Until the early 1960's, it was traditionally managed as a hay meadow and scythed once a year for fodder. With a new incumbent 'tidiness' was encouraged and the churchyard was mown on a regular basis but the cuttings were always removed. As a result, several unusual plants have survived.

In 1993, Warwickshire Wildlife Trust advised on a change in management. By 1998, the Churchyard received a grant from Rural Action for a full survey and management plan, a task carried out by Louise Slack from Warwickshire Museum who described it as one of the best pieces of grassland in the county. It contains a wealth of cowslip, betony, devil's-bit scabious, hoary plaintain, common birds-foot-trefoil, black knapweed, lady's mantle and common bistort. Grasses include oat-grass and quaking grass.

Because of the wide variety of plants and their different flowering times, management is carried out in compartments with constant monitoring. We typically take a hard cut to the churchyard at the beginning of the season as soon as it is dry enough. Thereafter some compartments are left uncut to allow grasses and earlier spring flowers such as cowslip, bugle and cuckooflower to flower and set seed, whilst other areas are cut at a height of three to four inches until the end of May. The latter provides a good showing of wildflowers because it still allows time for the betony, knapweed, birds-foot-trefoil, selfheal, hoary plaintain and devils-bit scabious to flower and set seed but it suppresses the grasses which people generally find so 'untidy'. The whole area is cut again in the autumn.

Oldberrow Church, Oldberrow — Keith Warrington

Getting the balance between allowing plants to flower and set seed for their long-term survival, and creating an acceptable appearance to those that live in the parish is a delicate and sensitive business. Keeping the locals informed of what's happening is not only courteous but it is an opportunity to explain the rarity and fragility of this kind of diminishing habitat and allows them to take an interest and a pride in preserving it. Putting up information boards to explain what you are doing helps to stop passers-by thinking the churchyard is neglected and describing it as 'disgraceful'. Parishioners at Oldberow have been very supportive of this project and we've never been short of help in the management.

Being such an excellent piece of top quality unimproved grassland the site is attractive to a variety of butterfly species. I have seen Ringlet, Meadow Brown, Gatekeeper, Skippers, Common Blue and even Marbled White.

Jane O'Dell

Lea Marston Churchyard
(SP205927)

The tiny churchyard at Lea Marston, near Coleshill is sheltered by surrounding trees and it's wild unimproved grassy vegetation often remains uncut through the summer when it becomes a haven for butterflies.

Meadow Brown, Gatekeeper and Skippers nectar on knapweed and betony and Holly Blue and Brimstone are regular spring visitors.

Keith Warmington

Brimstone *Gonepteryx rhamni*

The sulphur-yellow uppersides of the wings of the male Brimstone together with his strong flight are unmistakable. The female has paler, almost white wings and is often confused with the Large White though she has unmarked hooked wing-tips.

Brimstones always settle with their wings closed and when at rest amongst foliage are brilliantly concealed, especially when hibernating in dense ivy growth.

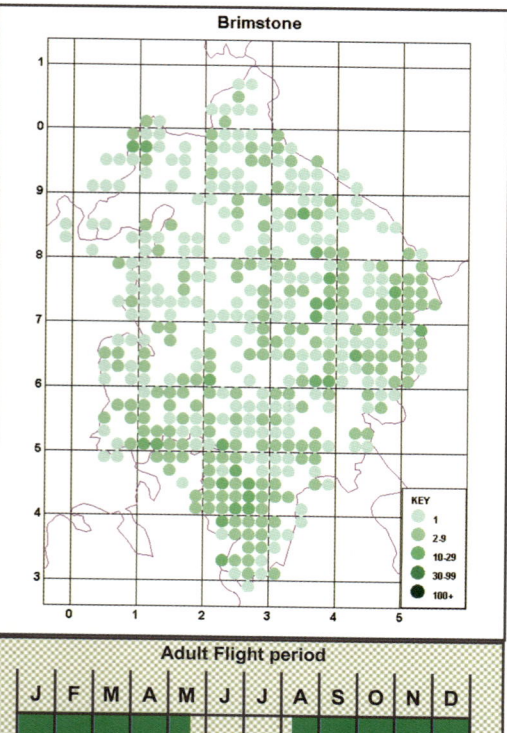

Holly Blue *Celastrina argiolus*

Common in Warwickshire.

The Holly Blue is easily identified in early spring, as it emerges well before other blue butterflies. The lilac-blue upperside of the wings of the male have thin black borders where the female has unmistakable broad black bands. The underside of both sexes is silvery-blue with speckles of black and no trace of orange.

Unlike most blues the Holly Blue is frequently seen flying high around bushes and trees.

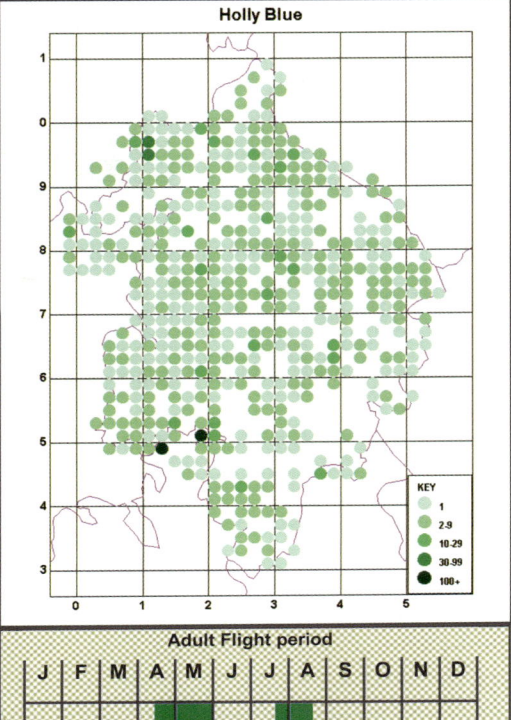

Adult Flight period

J	F	M	A	M	J	J	A	S	O	N	D
			■	■	■		■	■			

KEY: 1, 2-9, 10-29, 30-99, 100+

Additional Sites:

Alveston Churchyard, Alveston
(SP232564)

Unmown grass amongst grave stones.
Small Skipper, Brimstone, Holly Blue, Speckled Wood.

Gaydon Cemetery, Gaydon
(SP368537)

Wildflower hay meadow.
Large and Small Skipper, Common Blue, Meadow Brown.

London Road Cemetary, Coventry
(SP341783)

Large, mature, walled cemetery garden in urban setting with holly trees and shrubs.
Brimstone, Holly Blue, Speckled Wood, Small Tortoiseshell, Red Admiral, Gatekeeper.

Gaydon cemetery.

Industrial and Post-Industrial Landscape

Baddesley Colliery Site, baddesley Ensor — Keith Warmington

The impact of industry on the environment of both urban and rural districts of the Warwickshire area has been extensive. Sometimes this has been negative, resulting in pollution and unattractive dereliction. However, there have been some significant benefits for wildlife too - a legacy of many fantastic wildlife sites. The main categories of industrial and post industrial sites in the Warwickshire area are quarries, gravel pits, sand pits, collieries and areas of demolition. Many such sites are fully abandoned but even actively used sites such as Southam quarry, can support substantial interest where disturbance is only partial.

Colliery closures carried out between the 1960's and 1980's left a legacy of spoil heaps and derelict land containing waste materials mined

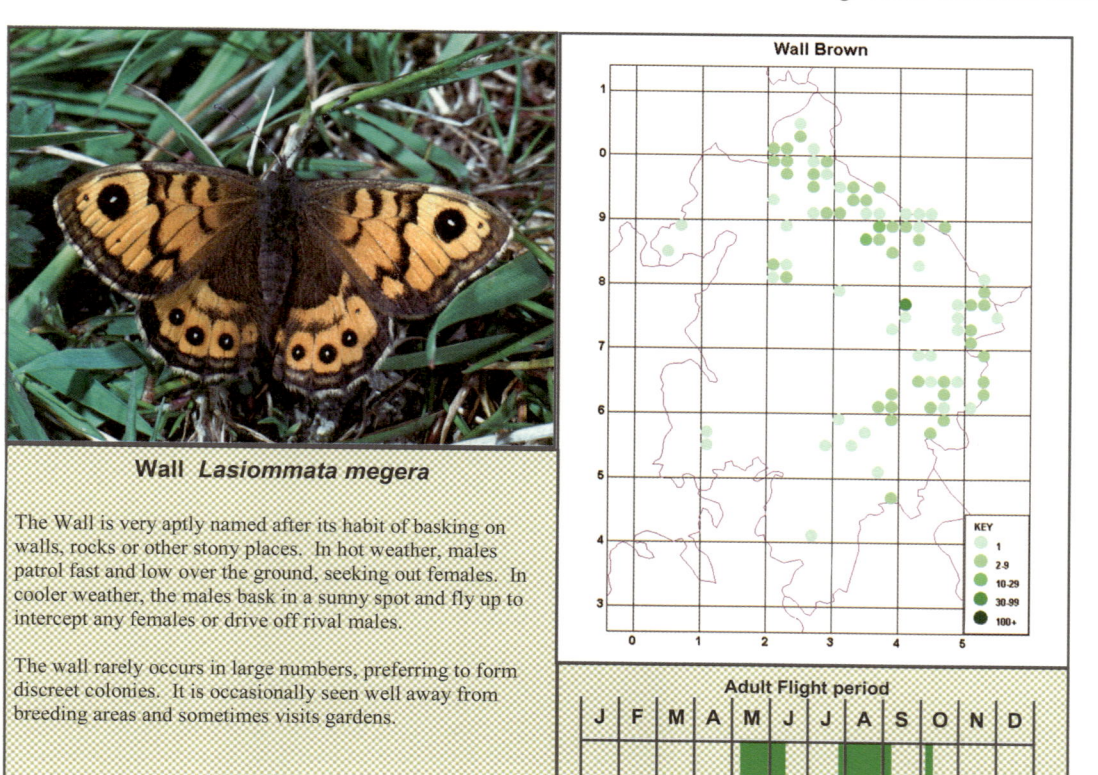

Wall *Lasiommata megera*

The Wall is very aptly named after its habit of basking on walls, rocks or other stony places. In hot weather, males patrol fast and low over the ground, seeking out females. In cooler weather, the males bask in a sunny spot and fly up to intercept any females or drive off rival males.

The wall rarely occurs in large numbers, preferring to form discreet colonies. It is occasionally seen well away from breeding areas and sometimes visits gardens.

Wall Brown

KEY: 1, 2-9, 10-29, 30-99, 100+

Adult Flight period

| J | F | M | A | M | J | J | A | S | O | N | D |

Dingy Skipper *Erynnis tages*

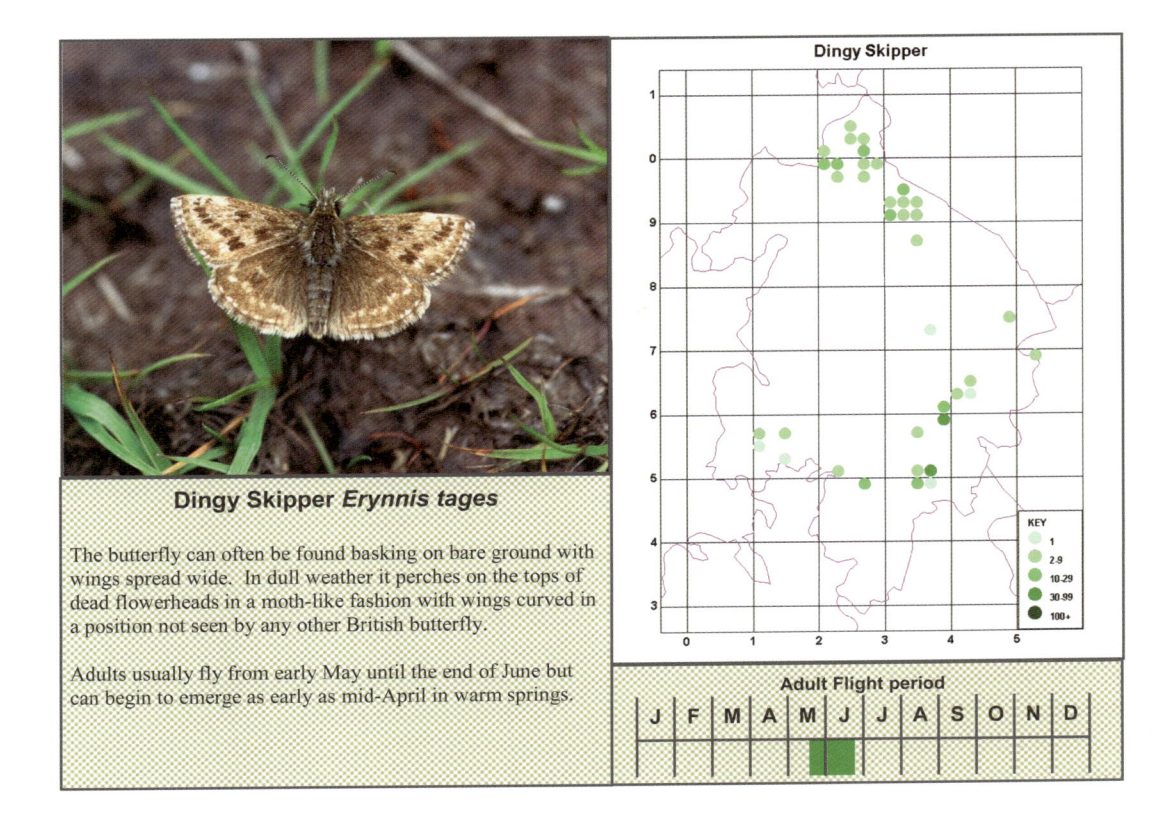

The butterfly can often be found basking on bare ground with wings spread wide. In dull weather it perches on the tops of dead flowerheads in a moth-like fashion with wings curved in a position not seen by any other British butterfly.

Adults usually fly from early May until the end of June but can begin to emerge as early as mid-April in warm springs.

from the ground and then left in huge tips. The spoil is usually acidic due to the mineral pyrite naturally present in the clay shales and may contain heavy metals. When left to re-vegetate naturally, such unpromising conditions can produce gems in wildlife terms. Many old abandoned tips in North Warwickshire now contain acid grassland with gorse, wavy hairgrass, bents and fescues. Small patches of heather may even be present. Spoilbanks have often become re-colonised by rough grassland and scrub. Characteristic flowers include birdsfoot trefoil, heath bedstraw, tormentil, knapweed and ragwort.

In the Rugby and Harbury areas several huge lias limestone quarries support some of our finest modern butterfly sites with strong populations of some of our rarest species. The dry, skeletal soils of the quarry sides and spoilheaps support much of Warwickshire's best limestone grassland, with many types of calcicolous' (lime-loving) plants. These include great knapweed, dwarf thistle, kidney vetch, wild basil, autumn gentian and many more.

Bishops Hill, Bishops Itchington.

Even more generalist plants such as birds-foot trefoil can exist at unusually high levels of abundance. These relatively recently formed habitats benefit butterflies for a number of reasons. Perhaps the most important factor is the abundance of certain larval foodplants. This is particularly true of the Small Blue which is confined to sheltered areas of Bishops Hill, Bishops Bowl and Southam Quarry where it's sole foodplant, kidney vetch grows in profusion.

Another important factor is the wealth of warm, south facing slopes associated with quarry faces and spoilheaps. The bare patches of ground here are important for Dingy Skipper and Wall. The variety of nectar plants for butterflies is probably greater than for any other habitat category.

Other types of limestone and ironstone quarry exist further south in the Edge Hill area, Napton and Cross Hands Quarry at the extreme southern tip of Warwickshire. They lack the richness of the lias quarries but are nevertheless important sites.

Unfortunately, most of our limestone quarries lack public access but occasionally host guided walks and owners may provide access with prior permission. Gems particularly worth seeking permits for include Bishops Bowl, Stockton Quarry and Cross Hands Quarry.

Unfortunately, industrial and post industrial sites largely fall within the category of previously-used or 'brown-field' land, which the Government is keen to develop in preference to 'green-field' land. It is important to note that all of Warwickshire's current Dingy Skipper and Small Blue sites are 'brown-field' ones, as well as the greater proportion of Grizzled Skipper, Green Hairstreak and Wall sites! The Ecologists of Coventry and Warwickshire Museum have made considerable efforts to highlight this issue and many good 'brown-field' sites are now designated as SINC's (Sites of Importance for Nature Conservation).

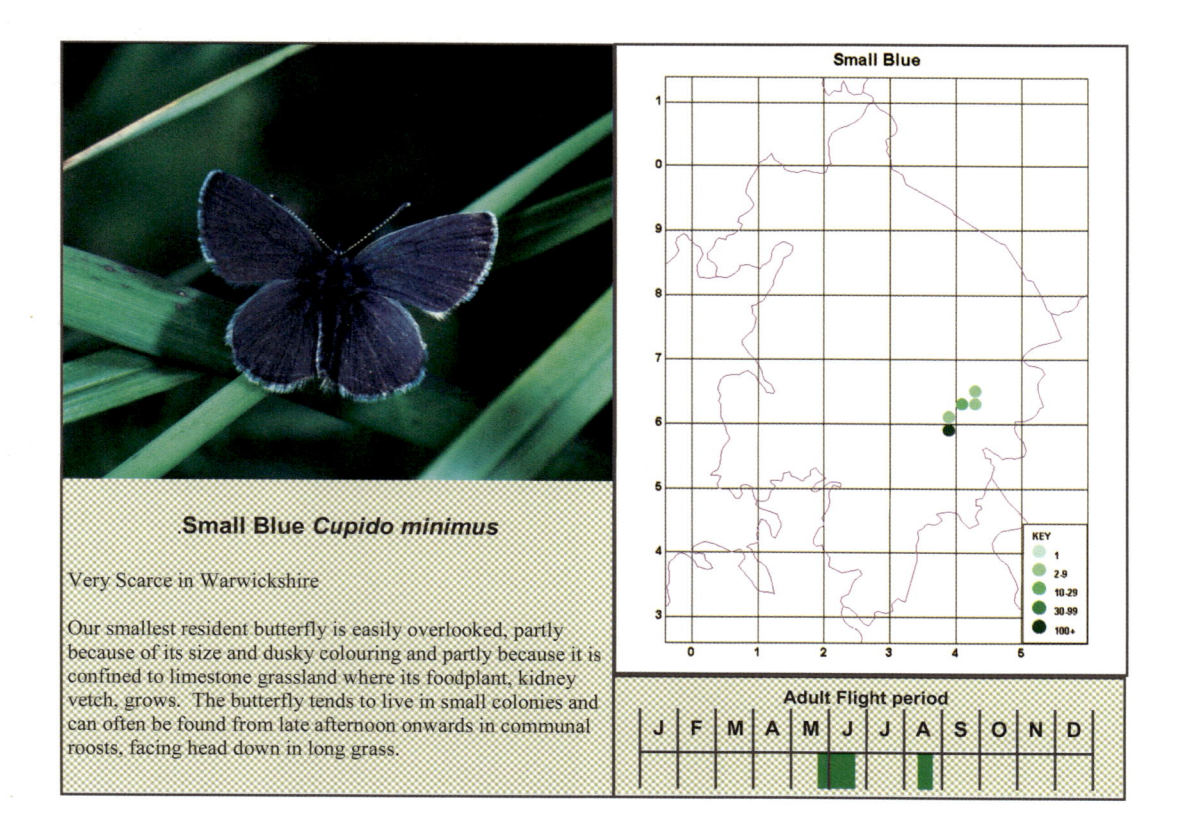

Small Blue *Cupido minimus*

Very Scarce in Warwickshire

Our smallest resident butterfly is easily overlooked, partly because of its size and dusky colouring and partly because it is confined to limestone grassland where its foodplant, kidney vetch, grows. The butterfly tends to live in small colonies and can often be found from late afternoon onwards in communal roosts, facing head down in long grass.

I had been visiting all of Warwickshire's larger limestone quarries since 1990 to record various groups of insects, most notably the flies, bees and wasps which produce some particularly rich and unusual assemblages in flowery limestone habitats. But in 2001 and 2002, special efforts were made to improve Warwickshire County Council's data for these sites and review their designations as wildlife sites. Many of the better quarries lack designation and, being brown-field land, a number are vulnerable to development.

Those two years will remain amongst my most satisfying periods as a naturalist. I had wonderful encounters with butterflies and tried to make time to appreciate these in between my intensive surveying of other insect groups. I observed Small Blue swarming at Bishops Hill and Southam Quarry, Grizzled and Dingy Skippers chasing each other at Southam and Harbury Spoilbank, the regular flashes of Green Hairstreak at Bishops Hill and Stockton Cutting, and a small colony of Wall at Southam Quarry (a butterfly that always takes me back to my childhood). Many of these quarries are amongst our most attractive wildlife sites, perhaps none more so than Bishops Bowl, where a rich mosaic of grasslands and wetlands are framed by cliffs of blue lias limestone – a legacy of our local cement industry.

And I added a hoverfly to the British list to boot and many other species to the Warwickshire list! Those two seasons reminded me of what a wonderful flagship group butterflies are. If we just secured the future of the Small Blue at its few modern sites, this alone would benefit so many other scarce insects and flowers by default.

Steven Falk

Recommended Sites:

Former Colliery Site, Baddesley Ensor
(SP272978)

Vegetative recolonisation of colliery spoilheaps and workings has produced suitable habitat for grassland species including Large and Small Skippers, Dingy Skipper, Common Blue and Small Heath. Wall and Green Hairstreak have been recorded in the past. A wooded path gives good numbers of Speckled Wood and Purple Hairstreaks.

The adjoining Grendon Common (SP280980), formerly an opencast mining site, also has Dingy Skipper, Ringlet, Common Blue and Small Heath.

Pooley Fields, Alvecote
(SK250044)

A woodland and wetland walk leads to the short grassy areas surrounding the spoilheap of a former colliery.

Birds-foot trefoil predominates and supports a large colony of Common Blue. Dingy Skipper, Small Copper and Small Heath are also common. A May walk can produce more than a dozen species of butterfly and at this time of year a number of dragonfly species including the rare Hairy Dragonfly are on the wing.

Bishops Hill, Bishops Itchington
(SP392584)

(See over.)

Bishops Hill SP392584

This hill consists of limestone waste from the local cement works. Although some 10 years ago it was bulldozed and lost much of its wildlife value it has made a wonderful recovery as far as butterflies are concerned.

It is a favoured spot on a sunny day and one can sit amongst the wild flowers watching many butterflies as well as having a good view over a large area of Warwickshire.

Keith Warmington

Bishops Hill, Bishops Itchington.

One warm afternoon in early September my companion and I had walked to the top of the hill disturbing many beautiful butterflies from the various wild flowers. Whilst sitting for a rest several species danced by including a number of Clouded Yellows.

When we came down the hill we had a bonus in the shape of a man-made beauty. I said to my friend " I can hear a Rolls Royce Merlin" and almost immediately a Spitfire flew over us!

Butterflies seen that day were Clouded Yellow, Small Tortoiseshell, Painted Lady, Red Admiral, Meadow Brown, Speckled Wood, Common Blue and Green-veined White.

This site is also the home of the Small Blue, Dingy and Grizzled Skippers, Brown Argus and Green Hairstreak as well as several day flying moths.

Phil Pain

DAY-FLYING MOTHS
BY
DAVID BROWN

Mother Shipton — *Keith Warmington*

Introduction

The separation of butterflies and moths is simply a division of convenience, for on a worldwide basis, there is no single feature separating all the butterflies from all the moths. However, the antennae are the most reliable aid to identification.

All the British butterflies have clubbed antennae whereas moth antennae narrow at the tip. The Burnets (*Zygaenidae*) possess antennae that are more similar to butterflies, being lobed but tapering at the very tip. The forewing and hindwing of moths are linked with a bristle or cluster of hairs called a frenulum which butterflies lack.

The general resting posture for butterflies (with the exception of the Dingy Skipper) is with wings tightly closed and held vertically above the body. Moths have a variety of resting positions and in the majority of macro-moths the wings cover the body. There are only a handful of moths which rest in butterfly fashion, one of which, the Bordered White, can be encountered flying in sunshine amongst Pine woodland.

In Warwickshire, there are over 30 species of macro moths that may be seen flying regularly during the daytime. The most likely to be confused with butterflies are the Burnets due to their bright red colours and lobed antennae. The resting posture with wings held flat down the line of the body is a useful identification aid.

Another frequent confusion occurs between the Grizzled Skipper and day flying moth species such as the Mother Shipton and Latticed Heath. The black and white chequered patterns of these species may cause difficulties when they are flying. Care must be taken to check the antennae.

Most spectacular of all day flying moths is the migratory Humming-bird Hawk-moth. It hovers over flowers darting around just like a tiny humming-bird and feeds on the wing, probing deep into flowers with its long proboscis. It is becoming a much more frequent visitor to Warwickshire and will often appear in gardens.

Scarlet Tiger — *Keith Warmington*

Woodland

Large Red-belted Clearwing Synanthedon culiciformis (Linn)

There are old records of this species from Clowes Wood, Wappenbury Wood, Oakley Wood, Princethorpe Wood, Mays Wood, Austy Wood, Bubbenhall Wood and Snitterfield Bushes. Recent sightings of this moth relate to Sutton Park. The moth benefits from birch stumps that have been cut within the previous three years which are utilised for egg laying and subsequent larval development. The newly emerged adults can be found on birch stumps in mornings during the first two weeks of May and later flying around birch trees.

David Brown

Oak Eggar Lasiocampa quercus (Linn)

Males of this species fly very rapidly and erratically on warm days in July and August. They are too quick to pursue and only rarely come to rest. The Oak Eggar can be seen in a wide range of habitats within the county from open grassland sites such as Ufton Fields to rides and clearings in ancient woodland as in Ryton Wood and on heathland in Sutton Park.

The foodplants of the Oak Eggar larvae include bramble, sallow, oak and blackthorn.

David Brown

Orange Underwing Archiearis parthenias (Linn)

A distinctive moth which can be seen in woodland rides and clearings during the first sunny days of March and into early April, often in the company of newly awakened Small Tortoiseshells, Peacocks and Brimstones. It has a rapid flight often around the tops of birch trees but occasionally, basking on the ground or feeding at sallow blossom. Found in a number of woodlands in VC38 but especially plentiful at Oakley Wood, Oversley Wood, Clowes Wood, Sutton Park and Wappenbury Wood.

The larvae feed on birch.

David Brown

Light Orange Underwing *Archiearis notha* (Hb)

Another Spring species often seen on sunny days between early April and the beginning of May. The best chance of seeing both species of Orange Underwing together is in the first week of April at Wappenbury Wood and Oversley Wood. As with Orange Underwing, it occasionally basks on the ground or settles to take moisture and nutrients from muddy woodland tracts, especially on sunny mornings following an April shower. Additional sites for this moth include Clowes Wood and Snitterfield Bushes.

The Light Orange Underwing is far less common nationally and locally due to its reliance upon aspen as a larval foodplant.

David Brown

Argent and Sable *Rheumaptera hastata* (Linn)

An attractive moth with a distinctive pattern of contrasting black and white markings, clearly visible in flight. The Argent and Sable is a priority species listed in the UK Biodiversity Action Plan. In Warwickshire, it is now only found in Hay Wood where it relies upon a continuous supply of young birch and can be seen flying on sunny or humid days in late May and June. Having disappeared from Austy Wood, Mays Wood, Brandon Wood, Bubbenhall Glade, Clowes Wood, Tile Hill Wood, Wappenbury Wood and Coughton Park since the 1950's and from Oversley Wood, Waverley Wood and Sutton Park since the 1970's, it is of paramount importance that sufficient regenerating birch is maintained through correct habitat management at its last remaining site.

Jim Porter

Bordered White *Bupalus piniaria* (Linn)

A common species most easily observed flying rapidly around the tree tops of well established pine plantations on hot sunny days in June and July. It is especially plentiful in Oversley Wood, Hay Wood and Waverley Wood and also Sutton Park.

The larvae feed on most species of pine through to September.

Jim Porter

The excitement of the second county sighting of the Red-necked Footman on 23 June 1996 resulted in a cricket match at Long Lawford, Rugby being halted! The umpire (IR), a keen Lepidopterist, recognised this distinctive black moth as it flew across the square. The stoppage continued whilst he emptied a packet of cigarettes on to the field and proceeded to place the moth into the empty box (for later verification), much to the amazement and subsequent amusement of the players.

Iain Reid

Red-necked Footman *Atolmis rubricollis* (Linn)

A species that flies both in sunshine and at night. Although there are currently only five records of this species in Warwickshire, there is evidence that it is becoming established within the county. The first sighting in our area was in Coventry on 10 July 1985, followed by a second on 23 June 1996 in Long Lawford (see anecdote). This species then occurred twice more in 2001, on 23 June at Shottery, Stratford on Avon and 26 June at Oversley Wood. The most recent record, again at Oversley Wood, was on 29th June 2002.

Jim Porter

The larvae feed on algae and lichens growing on trees such as oak, larch and pine.

Neutral and Acid Grassland

Narrow-bordered Five Spot Burnet *Zygaena lonicerae* (Schev)

Another species of Burnet moth which can be found in local abundance throughout Warwickshire in a wider range of habitats than Six-spot Burnet such as road and railway cuttings, old quarries, gravel pits, woodland clearings, rides and wetlands. Single brooded, it flies in the last two weeks of June and throughout July. Recommended sites include Ryton Pool Country Park, Alvecote Pools, Stonebridge Meadows and Ettington Road Cutting.

Jim Porter

The larvae feed on clovers, vetches and trefoils.

Chimney Sweeper *Odezia atrata* (Linn)

This attractive little moth with subtle white wing tips can form conspicuous colonies in meadows and other grassy areas throughout the county where the larval foodplant pignut grows. It has a lazy fluttering flight and frequently settles on grass and plant stems. The adult has been noted in Warwickshire from early June to late July in areas such as Stonebridge Meadows, Charlecote and Whittleford Park.

Jim Porter

Latticed Heath *Chiasmia clathrata* (Linn)

A very common species using a wide range of grassland types throughout Warwickshire. It may be observed almost continuously throughout the summer as there are two broods; firstly in May and June and again in July to September. Typical sites include Ufton Fields and Windmill Hill, Nuneaton.

The larvae feed on clovers and trefoils.

David Brown

Cinnabar *Tyria jacobaeae* (Linn)

A well known species to butterfly enthusiasts as this moth can often be seen during the summer months whilst butterfly watching. It can be found anywhere where there is a good growth of groundsel or ragwort and has been regularly recorded by observers in Leamington, Rugby, Coventry and Birmingham. This species is found over a wide area in VC38 including Bishops Hill, Ryton Pool Country Park and Brandon Marsh.

The yellow and black banded larvae are just as familiar a sight as the adult moth as they feed on ragwort.

David Brown

Small Yellow Underwing *Panemeria tenebrata* (Scop)

One of the smallest British species of macro moth and one which could easily be mistaken for a pyralid micro-moth species when on the wing. It flies on sunny days in May and early June amongst flowers in grassy meadows, disused railway embankments, old quarries and open areas in woodland. Despite its small size, this species is recorded in the county from over forty locations including Navigation Cutting and Edgehill.

The larval foodplant is common mouse-ear.

Jim Porter

Mother Shipton *Callistege mi* (cl)

This attractive moth is occasionally confused with the Grizzled Skipper butterfly. It occurs in a wide range of grassy habitats including wide woodland rides such as in Brandon Wood and Ryton Wood and heathland such as Grendon Common and Sutton Park. However it is most frequent in disused railway cuttings and in old quarries.

The larvae feed on clovers and birds-foot trefoil.

David Brown

Limestone Grassland

Forester *Adscita statices* (Linn)

This attractive green moth has disappeared from a number of locations in Warwickshire during the last 50 years. It is now only found at Ashlawn Railway Cutting NR where Butterfly Conservation annually monitors numbers of the adult during June and early July. In 1997, a taskforce was initiated to carry out a programme of scrub clearance each winter. This work has created larger areas of suitable open grassland where the larval foodplant, common sorrel, can flourish. It has been a successful operation to date, clearly improving the Forester population.

David Brown

Six-spot Burnet *Zygaena filipendulae* (Linn)

This bright red spotted moth is conspicuous in the company of grassland butterflies during July and early August. It is especially common on calcareous grassland on disused railway cuttings where birds-foot trefoil (the larval foodplant) grows though it will occur on other grassland types. It is particularly common at Navigation Cutting, Grove Hill, Bishops Hill and Ufton Fields where adults can be observed at leisure as they take nectar from knapweed and thistle flowers.

David Brown

Orange-tailed Clearwing *Synanthedon andrenaeformis* (Lasp)

This moth was only added to the Warwickshire list in 2001 when half a dozen larval caps were noted on wayfaring tree at Burton Dassett Hills Country Park. From a retained section of stem, a male emerged on 12 June. Detailed searches for the moth during June or for the earlier stages on wayfaring trees situated on limestone soils may bring further colonies to our notice.

David Brown

Six-belted Clearwing *Bembecia ichneumoniformis* (D&S)

This moth is usually observed flying low close to birds-foot trefoil plants on warm sunny days. By late afternoon the adults stop flying and rest upon the trefoil plants. Warwickshire strongholds for this moth are disused railway lines such as Ashlawn Cutting NR, Navigation and Stockton Cutting; also old quarries such as Stockton; post industrial sites such as Pooley Fields, Alvecote and some roadside verges. It is on the wing from mid-June to the start of August.

Jim Porter

Burnet Companion *Euclidia glyphica* (Linn)

On the wing in late May and June, this moth can often be seen on grassy embankments on calcareous soils, often in the company of the Mother Shipton. Both are particularly plentiful at Bishops Hill and Ashlawn Railway Cutting. Burnet Companion adults are very active and easily disturbed at which time they embark on a short rapid flight before resettling.

The larvae feed chiefly on birds-foot trefoil and clovers.

David Brown

Small Purple-barred *Phytometra vividaria* (cl)

A small easily overlooked species which flies from late May to July. It travels rapidly for short distances and frequently settles on bare earth. This moth is presently known at only two privately owned sites in Warwickshire (both without access) but with more detailed searches of sites where common milkwort the larval foodplant occurs, it may prove to be more widespread.

David Brown

Wetlands

Lunar Hornet Moth *Sesia bembeciformis* (Hb)

This wasp-like moth can be seen in the vicinity of sallow bushes in damp habitats during July. Newly emerged moths may be found drying their wings on the sallow trunks in the mornings. Very local in Warwickshire with only four sites presently known. The largest colony is adjacent to the car park at Ryton Organic Gardens and was discovered when some trees were felled in 1999 revealing larval tunnels in the stems.

David Brown

Red-tipped Clearwing *Synanthedon formicaeformis* (Esp)

Although this species was recorded from Sutton Park in 1891, it is now only seen at Brandon Marsh. A very elusive moth and possibly under-recorded. It can be observed on osier, willow and sallow (the larval foodplants) or occasionally at ground level feeding at various flowers.

David Brown

Marsh Pug *Eupithecia pygmaeata* (Hb)

This tiny moth goes unnoticed by all except the keenest of observers and so far only eight Warwickshire sites are known including Whitacre Heath and Charlecote. It flies during May and June in damp meadows where the larval foodplant field mouse-ear grows.

David Brown

Scarlet Tiger *Callimorpha dominula* (Linn)

This striking moth flies by day and night. It's favourite habitat is marshy ground near streams where there is a good growth of comfrey. However, in Warwickshire, the two most recent recordings have been in gardens at Rugby in 1997 and nearby, Marton in 2001 where other herbaceous plants are used.

David Brown

Gardens and Parks

Currant Clearwing *Synanthedon tipuliformis* (cl)

This small Clearwing is a rapid flyer and difficult to follow as it skips and darts over currant and gooseberry bushes in late morning sunshine during June and early July. It is easier to observe after 4pm when adults tend to rest on the leaves. At present the only known colonies occur in the gardens of moth enthusiasts at Marton, Pillerton Priors, Charlecote, Leamington, Coventry, Birmingham and Water Orton. There must surely be many undiscovered colonies throughout the county.

Jim Porter

Red-belted Clearwing *Synanthedon myopaeformis* (Borkh)

An elusive Clearwing which utilises crab apple, pear, almond, cherry and other trees in gardens old orchards and tree lined roads. It is rarely seen in Warwickshire but careful searching for exit holes in the bark of suitable trees in June and July could produce further locations.

David Brown

Humming-bird Hawk-moth *Macroglossum stellatarum* (Linn)

Many people genuinely think they have seen a humming-bird when they first encounter this moth. It feeds on flowers such as buddleia, valerian, honeysuckle, petunia or jasmine and frequently visits gardens. In the past two decades this migrant species has become a regular visitor to a wide range of Warwickshire habitats.

David Brown

Vapourer *Orgyia antiqua* (Linn)

A common and widespread species occurring in a variety of habitats. The females are wingless but the tawny coloured males may be seen flying erratically in gardens, parks and woodland in sunshine from July to late September. This species may also be very common in urban areas and reached plague proportions in Coventry city centre in July 1975.

The larvae have spectacular hair tufts and feed on many tree and shrub species including birch, oak, lime, hawthorn and blackthorn.

Jim Porter

Silver Y *Autographa gamma* (Linn)

This common migrant can be observed flying during the daytime in almost every part of the county. Gardens provide a good source of nectar and 'swarms' of Silver Y moths may occasionally be observed hovering over beds of valerian or around buddliea flowers.

The larvae feed on a tremendous variety of plants and can be a pest on vegetables.

David Brown

Heathland

Emperor Moth *Saturnia pavonia* (Linn)

This fine insect is most easily seen in Sutton Park where the males fly rapidly and erratically over heather in sunshine during late April and throughout May. It has been recorded in other parts of the county in the past and disused railway lines provide suitable conditions for a few small colonies.

The larvae feed on a variety of plants such as hawthorn, bramble, sallow, meadow sweet and heather.

David Brown

Common Heath *Ematurga atomaria* (Linn)

This heath and downland species is restricted to Sutton Park and a few railway cuttings on limestone soil in the south of the county. It flies from late May until August.

The larval foodplants are heather, trefoils and clovers.

Jim Porter

Beautiful Yellow Underwing *Anarta myrtilli* (Linn)

This heathland species has only been recorded in Sutton Park, where it flies rapidly over areas of heather in hot sunshine. There are two overlapping broods and it has been observed from mid May to mid August.

The larval foodplants are heather and bell heather.

Jim Porter

North American Indian legend holds that when the Great Spirit created the world he lined the stream beds with pebbles of every colour. He decided these were not visible enough and called in the South Wind to breathe life into the stones. When he did so they rose and flew - jewels in the sky.

These were the first butterflies and moths.

Appendix One

Distribution Status of Butterflies in Warwickshire

The following table shows the number of tetrads (2km x 2km squares) that each of the Warwickshire butterfly species were found in during the 'Millennium Atlas' Survey 1995-1999. The total number of tetrads surveyed was 705. The table is arranged to show the most widespread species at the top.

Species	Tetrads
Gatekeeper	699
Meadow Brown	699
Green-veined White	698
Orange Tip	696
Small Tortoiseshell	691
Small White	689
Peacock	688
Speckled Wood	668
Small Skipper	650
Large White	650
Large Skipper	592
Ringlet	541
Red Admiral	498
Holly Blue	490
Comma	440
Brimstone	428
Painted Lady	401
Common Blue	390
Small Copper	318
Small Heath	207
Purple Hairstreak	197
Marbled White	168
Brown Argus	113
White-letter Hairstreak	108
Wall	88
Clouded Yellow	65
Essex Skipper	62
Grizzled Skipper	43
Dingy Skipper	38
White Admiral	38
Green Hairstreak	16
Camberwell Beauty	13
Silver Washed Fritillary	10
Small Blue	5
Wood White	3
Dark Green Fritillary	3
Total Recorded Squares	705

Appendix Two

Butterfly Plants

Ash *(Fraxinus excelsior)*	10 29
Aubretia *(Aubretia deltoidea)*	47
Birds-foot-trefoil *(Lotus corniculatus)*	18 21 34 42 51 55 56 47
Blackthorn *(Prunus spinosa)*	30 35
Bramble *(Rubus fruticosus agg.)*	8 9 11 12 30 35 49 50
Buckthorn *(Rhamnus cathartica)*	10 25 30 42
Buddleia *(Buddleja spp.)*	31 42 43 46 47
Bugle *(Ajuga reptans)*	34 51
Coltsfoot *(Tussilago farfara)*	35
Cuckooflower *(Cardamine pratensis)*	21 36 51
Devil's-bit scabious *(Succisa pratensis)*	19 51
Doves-foot cranesbill *(Geranium molle)*	6
Echinops	47
Elm *(Ulmus spp.)*	5 8 16 25 29 37 42
Escallonia bifida	46
Eupatorium see Hemp agrimony	
Fleabane (common) *(Palicaria dysenterica)*	43
Garlic mustard *(Alliaria petiolata)*	21 30 42
Hemp agrimony *(Eupatorium cannabinum)*	21 47
Holly *(Ilex aquifolium)*	10 29 47 50 53
Honeysuckle *(Lonicera periclymenum)*	9 11 12 15 47
Ice plant see Sedum	
Ivy *(Hedera helix)*	29 42 43 47 50 52
Kidney vetch *(Anthyllis vulneraria)*	5 20 22 55 56
Knapweed (Centaurea spp.)	20 36 39 51 55
Lady's smock see Cuckooflower	
Lavender *(Lavandula angustifolia)*	46 47
Marjoram *(Oreganum vulgare)*	20 43 46 47
Michaelmas daisy *(Aster novo-blgii)*	46 47
Nettles see Stinging nettles	
Oak *(Quercus spp.)*	5 10 11 14 15 29 47
Oregano see Marjoram	
Purple loosestrife *(Lythrum salicaria)*	21
Rock rose *(Helianthemum)*	6
Sallow *(Salix spp.)*	12 30
Scabious (field) *(Knautia arvensis)*	46 47
Sedum *(Sedum spectabile)*	46 47
Sorrel *(Rumex spp)*	42
Stinging nettles *(Urtica dioica)*	5 21 25 42 45 50
Strawberry (wild) *(Fragaria vesca)*	5 34
Sweet rocket *(Hesperis matronalis)*	43
Thistle *(Cirsium spp.)*	20 25 36 55
Thyme *(Thymus)*	47
Valerian *(Centranthus)*	47
Verbena *(Verbena)*	47
Verbena bonariensis	43
Violet *(Viola* spp.)	8 9 11 13
Wallflower (Bowles purple) *(Erysimum)*	43
Yorkshire fog *(Holcus lanatus)*	42

Appendix Three

Gazetteer

The following list gives a six-figure Ordnance Survey map reference for all sites mentioned in the book. Details on how to read grid references are shown on all Ordnance Survey maps.

Site	Grid Ref	Pages
Abbey Fields	SP287724	45
Alvecote Pools	SK250044	63
Alveston Churchyard	SP232564	53
Ashlawn Railway Cutting NR	SP517732	35 36 37 38 39 65 66 67
Baddesley Ensor (Old Colliery)	SP272978	57
Bishops Hill	SP392584	56 57 58 64 66 67
Bishops Bowl	SP389588	56
Brandon Marsh NR	SP386761	3 64 68
Brandon Wood	SP39971	10 14 62 65
Burton Dassett Hills CP	SP392520	66
Castle Hills	SP177822	24
Castle Lane	SP226902	32
Charlecote	SP263577	64 68 69
Clowes Wood	SP102744	61 62
Crackley Wood LNR	SP289739	10 45
Crimscote	SP236472	32
Deans Green LNR	SP132682	19
Dordon Lane	SP226902	32
Draycote Meadow NR	SP448706	3 19
Draycote Reservoir	SP468692	3
Eathorpe NR	SP389687	3 24
Edgehill	SP367473	65
Ettington	SP264492	31 63
Fulready	SP294453	32
Gaydon Cemetery	SP368537	53
Glasshouse Lane	SP303726	31
Greenway (The)	SP196540	39
Grendon Common	SP280980	57 65
Grove Hill	SP112547	16 66
Hampton Wood NR	SP254600	2 13
Harborough Magna	see Pailton	
Harbury Spoilbank NR	SP384598	22 23 57
Hartshill Hayes CP	SP317943	10 14
Harvest Hill NR	SP279823	19
Hay Wood	SP205712	62
Henley Sidings	SP147669	38
Jephson Gardens	SP321657	44 46
Kenilworth Common LNR	SP297730	45
Kingfisher Pool	SP288648	44
Kingsbury Water Park	SP204960	3
Knowle Hill LNR	SP298728	24 45
Lake View CP	SP315795	46 47

Lea Marston Churchyard	SP205927	52
Leam Fields	SP333658	44
London Road Cemetary	SP341783	53
Middleton Hall	SP192981	48
National Herb Centre	SP411471	48
Navigation Cutting	SP524663	65 66
Newbold Lane	see Crimscote	
Newton Railway Cutting	SP529785	35 36 39
Oakley Wood	SP305596	61
Oldberrow Churchyard	SP121660	51
Oversley Wood	SP105563	11 15 16 61 62 63
Pagets Lane	SP373720	32
Pailton	SP477805	32
Parliament Piece	SP289729	45
Pooley Fields NR	SK258044	57 66
Ryton Organic Gardens	SP400746	48 67
Ryton Pools CP	SP374725	63 64
Ryton Wood NR	SP384726	2 9 10 13 61 65
Saltisford Common	SP273657	45
Shadowbrook	SP187814	19
Snitterflied Bushes LNR	SP200603	11 13 14 61 62
St Mary's Land	SP275649	44
Stonebridge Meadows LNR	SP327756	19 63 64
Stockton Cutting LNR	SP437651	23 45 57 66
Stratford Butterfly Farm	SP204546	47
Sutton Park	SP103966	3 10 19 61 62 65 68 70 71
Temple Balsall NR	SP203760	3
Ufton Fields LNR/CP	SP378615	22 23 64 66
Wappenbury Wood NR	SP381711	10 14 61 62
Waverley Wood	SP352709	62
Weddington Old Railway Line	SP359943	38
Welches Meadow LNR	SP325657	3 24 45
Whatcote Lane	see Fulready	
Whichford Wood	SP343296	11 14
Whitacre Heath NR	SP209931	3 68
Whitnash Brook	SP334637	44
Whittleford Park	SP335923	64
Windmill Hill	SP341932	64

PLEASE NOTE

No right of public access should be assumed to any of the sites mentioned in this list.

Appendix Four
Butterfly Conservation

Butterfly Conservation is the largest insect conservation body in the world and is devoted to the conservation of our native butterflies and moths, and their habitats. It is dynamic, fast growing and influential and its activities span all spheres of conservation work.

Over the last thirty years Butterfly Conservation has identified the species of butterfly that are most threatened and has produced Action Plans for their conservation. These Action Plans have influenced Government, both national and local, and land owners, and have helped to protect and restore the vital habitats that support butterflies and moths. Advice is given to land owners and managers on conserving and restoring important habitats.

Surveys are carried out together with monitoring and other essential research and the results are used to lobby government to improve land use policy.

Butterfly Conservation has over thirty reserves that are managed specifically as habitat for butterflies and moths. The Warwickshire branch is about to obtain the first reserve to be managed specifically for butterflies and moths in the county.

'Action for Butterflies', a conservation programme to save threatened butterflies includes a project to reintroduce the Large Blue, which became extinct in the UK in 1979. Working closely with other organisations Butterfly Conservation has successfully restored this beautiful butterfly to a number of sites.

The Warwickshire branch is one of over 30 branches of Butterfly Conservation run by volunteers in the UK. We work to conserve and increase the butterflies within the old county of Warwickshire (includes Coventry, Solihull, Sutton Coldfield and parts of the eastern Birmingham region). We carry out practical conservation work, surveys and monitoring, as well as campaigning to protect valuable habitats. During the butterfly season we run a series of butterfly walks and moth nights, where members, both new and old, can learn more about the butterflies and moths in our county from expert leaders. We also hold social events.

For more information contact either of the addresses below or visit the Butterfly Conservation web site at www.butterfly-conservation.org.

Butterfly Conservation
Manor Yard
East Lulworth
Wareham
Dorset, BH20 5QP

Telephone: 01929 400209
Email: info@butterfly-conservation.org

Warwickshire Branch of Butterfly Conservation
3 The Deer Leap
Kenilworth
Warwickshire
CV8 2HW

Appendix Five
Further Information

Organisations

Warwickshire Wildlife Trust
Brandon marsh Nature Centre
Brandon Lane
Coventry
CV3 3GW

Tel. 024 7630 2912
www.warwickshire-wildlife-trust.org.uk

The National Trust
West Midlands Regional Office
Attingham Park
Shrewsbury
SY4 4TP

Tel. 01743 708100
www.nationaltrust.org.uk

Warwickshire Museum
Market Place
Warwick
CV34 4SA

Tel. 01926 412500
www.warwickshire.gov.uk

The Country Park Information Centre
Kingsbury Water Park
Bodymoor Heath
Sutton Coldfield
B76 0DY

Tel. 01827 872660
www.warwickshire.gov.uk

Recommended Books

Asher J et al
The Millenium Atlas of Butterflies in Britain and Ireland
Oxford University Press, 2002

Tomlinson D and Still R
Britain's Butterflies
Wild Guides Ltd, 2002

Thomas J and Lewington R
The Butterflies of Britain and Ireland
Dorling Kinderlsey, 1991

Vickery M
Gardening for Butterflies
Butterfly Conservation, 1998

Barnett L and Emms C
Exploring Warwickshire's Wild Places
S.B. Publications, 1998

Tasker A (ed)
The Nature of Warwickshire
Barracuda Books Limited, 1990

Index of Warwickshire's Butterflies

Brimstone	5 15 25 28 31 32 35 38 41 42 44 45 46 47 48 50 **52** 53 61	*JR*
Brown Argus	6 15 *19* <u>26</u> 43 44 45 47 58	*JR*
Clouded Yellow	*32* 38 47 58	*JR*
Comma	5 *12* 15 25 32 35 41 42 43 45 46	*JR*
Common Blue	<u>5</u> 15 *18* 20 24 25 <u>26</u> 30 31 32 36 38 39 41 42 43 44 47 48 52 53 57 58	*KW*
Dark Green Fritillary	25	*JR*
Dingy Skipper	iii 4 13 15 20 22 23 35 45 **55** 56 57 58 60	*KW*
Essex Skipper	13 24 30 32 **36** 43 48	*JR*
Gatekeeper	5 15 25 **28** 30 31 32 38 39 41 42 43 46 47 50 52 53	*KW*
Green Hairstreak	iii 4 19 20 22 23 **35** 45 56 57 58	*JR*
Green-veined White	5 15 21 **22** 25 30 31 32 41 42 46 47 58	*JR*
Grizzled Skipper	<u>5</u> 14 15 20 22 23 **34** 35 45 56 57 58 60 65	*JR*
Hedge Brown	see Gatekeeper	
Holly Blue	5 15 24 29 32 39 41 42 43 45 46 47 48 50 52 **53**	*JR*
Large Skipper	5 15 18 24 25 31 32 33 36 **37** 39 41 43 44 45 46 47 50 53 57	*JR*
Large White	5 15 25 31 32 41 **43** 46 47	*JR*
Marbled White	5 13 16 **20** 22 23 24 25 30 31 32 38 39 41 43 44 45 47 50 52	*KW*
Meadow Brown	5 15 18 19 **23** 25 28 30 31 32 39 41 42 43 44 45 46 47 50 52 53 58	*JR*
Orange Tip	3 5 15 **21** 28 30 31 32 36 39 41 42 43 46 47	*JR*
Painted Lady	5 16 25 **33** 41 47 58	*JR*
Peacock	5 15 16 25 31 32 35 **40** 41 44 46 47 50 61	*KW*
Purple Hairstreak	1 5 *10* 11 13 14 15 24 29 32 39 43 45 48 57	*JR*
Red Admiral	5 15 41 42 **45** 46 47 50 53 58	*KW*
Ringlet	5 *13* 15 24 31 32 38 39 41 42 44 45 47 52 57	*JR*
Silver-washed Fritillary	2 5 *7* **8** 9 13 14 43 48	*JR*
Small Blue	iii 4 5 20 22 45 **56** 57 58	*JR*
Small Copper	15 19 **24** 32 36 38 39 41 42 43 44 45 47 48 57	*JR*
Small Heath	19 22 24 25 **31** 32 36 38 39 41 44 45 47 48 50 57	*JR*
Small Skipper	5 15 18 24 25 **30** 31 32 36 41 44 45 47 48 50 53 57	*JR*
Small Tortoiseshell	15 16 25 31 32 35 41 42 44 **46** 47 50 53 57 58 61	*JR*
Small White	5 15 25 31 32 33 **41** 46 47	*JR*
Speckled Wood	5 15 25 30 31 36 38 41 42 43 46 47 **50** 53 57 58	*JR*
Wall	4 19 22 38 39 41 47 48 **54** 56 57	*JR*
White Admiral	5 *9* 11 13 <u>14</u> 15	*JR*
White-letter Hairstreak	iii 1 5 13 14 16 24 25 **29** 31 32 37	*KW*
Wood White	*11* 14	*KW*

Additional Species

Camberwell Beauty	<u>48</u>	Pearl-bordered Fritillary	5	
Duke of Burgandy Fritillary	<u>6</u>	Small Pearl-bordered Fritillary	5 <u>6</u>	
Silver-studded Blue	3			

Initials indicate photographer of main entry species photograph.
JR = John Roberts and ***KW*** = Keith Warmington

Index of Warwickshire's Day-Flying Moths

Argent & Sable	*62*
Beautiful Yellow Underwing	*71*
Bordered White	60 *62*
Burnet Companion	*67*
Chimney Sweeper	45 *64*
Cinnabar	47 *64*
Common Heath	*71*
Currant Clearwing	*69*
Emperor Moth	*70*
Forester	38 *65*
Humming-bird Hawk-moth	60 *69*
Large Red-belted Clearwing	*61*
Latticed Heath	60 *64*
Light Orange Underwing	*62*
Lunar Hornet Moth	*67*
Marsh Pug	*68*
Mother Shipton	<u>59</u> 60 *65* 67
Narrow-bordered Five Spot Burnet	*63*
Oak Eggar	*61*
Orange-tailed Clearwing	*66*
Orange Underwing	*61* 62
Red-belted Clearwing	*69*
Red-Necked Footman	*63*
Red-tipped Clearwing	*68*
Scarlet Tiger	<u>60</u> *68*
Silver Y	*70*
Six-belted Clearwing	*66*
Six Spot Burnet	63 *66*
Small Purple-barred	*67*
Small Yellow Underwing	*65*
Vapourer	*70*

Index entries in ***bold italic*** indicate the main entry including photograph. <u>Underlined</u> indicates other photographs.

A Checklist of the Butterflies of Warwickshire

Common Name	Latin Name	☐	Location	Date
Small Skipper	*Thymelicus sylvestris*	☐		
Essex Skipper	*Thymelicus lineola*	☐		
Large Skipper	*Ochlodes venata*	☐		
Dingy Skipper	*Erynnis tages*	☐		
Grizzled Skipper	*Pyrgus malvae*	☐		
Wood White	*Leptidea sinapis*	☐		
Clouded Yellow	*Colias croceus*	☐		
Brimstone	*Gonepteryx rhamni*	☐		
Large White	*Pieris brassicae*	☐		
Small White	*Pieris rapae*	☐		
Green-veined White	*Pieris napi*	☐		
Orange Tip	*Anthocharis cardamines*	☐		
Green Hairstreak	*Callophrys rubi*	☐		
Purple Hairstreak	*Neozephyrus quercus*	☐		
White-letter Hairstreak	*Satyrium w-album*	☐		
Small Copper	*Lycaena phlaeas*	☐		
Small Blue	*Cupido minimus*	☐		
Brown Argus	*Aricia agestis*	☐		
Common Blue	*Polyommatus icarus*	☐		
Holly Blue	*Celastrina argiolus*	☐		
White Admiral	*Limenitis camilla*	☐		
Red Admiral	*Vanessa atalanta*	☐		
Painted Lady	*Cynthia cardui*	☐		
Small Tortoiseshell	*Aglais urticae*	☐		
Peacock	*Inachis io*	☐		
Comma	*Polygonia c-album*	☐		
Dark Green Fritillary	*Argynnis aglaja*	☐		
Silver-washed Fritillary	*Argynnis paphia*	☐		
Speckled Wood	*Pararge aegeria*	☐		
Wall	*Lasiommata megera*	☐		
Marbled White	*Melanargia galathea*	☐		
Gatekeeper	*Pyronia tithonus*	☐		
Meadow Brown	*Maniola jurtina*	☐		
Ringlet	*Aphantopus hyperantus*	☐		
Small Heath	*Coenonympha pamphilus*	☐		

A Checklist of the Day-flying Moths of Warwickshire

Common Name	Latin Name		Location	Date
Small Purple-barred	*Phytometra viridaria*	☐		
Forester	*Adscita statices*	☐		
Six Spot Burnet	*Zygaena filipendulae*	☐		
Narrow-bordered Five Spot Burnet	*Zygaena lonicerae*	☐		
Lunar Hornet Moth	*Sesia bembeciformis*	☐		
Currant Clearwing	*Synanthedon tipuliformis*	☐		
Orange-tailed Clearwing	*Syanthedon andrenaeformis*	☐		
Red-belted Clearwing	*Synanthedon myopaeformis*	☐		
Red-tipped Clearwing	*Synanthedon formicaeformis*	☐		
Large Red-belted Clearwing	*Synanthedon culiciformis*	☐		
Six-belted Clearwing	*Bembecia ichneumoniformis*	☐		
Oak Eggar	*Lasiocampa quercus*	☐		
Emperor Moth	*Saturnia pavonia*	☐		
Orange Underwing	*Archiearis parthenias*	☐		
Light Orange Underwing	*Archiearis notha*	☐		
Argent and Sable	*Rheumaptera hastata*	☐		
Marsh Pug	*Eupithecia pygmaeata*	☐		
Chimney Sweeper	*Odezia atrata*	☐		
Latticed Heath	*Chiasnia clathrata*	☐		
Common Heath	*Ematurga atomaria*	☐		
Bordered White	*Bupalus piniaria*	☐		
Humming-bird Hawk Moth	*Macroglossum stellatarum*	☐		
Vapourer	*Orgyia antiqua*	☐		
Red-necked Footman	*Atolmis rubricollis*	☐		
Scarlet Tiger	*Callimorpha dominula*	☐		
Cinnabar	*Tyria jacobaeae*	☐		
Beautiful Yellow Underwing	*Anarta myrtilli*	☐		
Small Yellow Underwing	*Panemeria tenebrata*	☐		
Silver Y	*Autographa gamma*	☐		
Mother Shipton	*Callistege mi*	☐		
Burnet Companion	*Euclidia glyphica*	☐		